THE WORD MADE FLESH

FOUNDATIONS OF CATHOLIC THEOLOGY SERIES

Gerard S. Sloyan, *Editor*

THE WORD MADE FLESH

DAVID J. BOWMAN, SJ

The Catholic University of America
Washington, D.C.

PRENTICE-HALL, INC.
Englewood Cliffs, N.J.

1963

Imprimi potest:

> John R. Connery, SJ
> Provincial, Chicago Province
> December 20, 1962

Nihil obstat:

> Eamon R. Carroll, O Carm, STD
> Censor Deputatus

Imprimatur:

> ✠ Patrick A. O'Boyle, DD
> Archbishop of Washington
> December 21, 1962

The *nihil obstat* and *imprimatur* are official declarations that a book or pamphlet is free of doctrinal or moral error. No implication is contained therein that those who have granted the *nihil obstat* and *imprimatur* agree with the content, opinions, or statements expressed.

PRENTICE-HALL INTERNATIONAL, INC., *London*
PRENTICE-HALL OF AUSTRALIA, PTY., LTD., *Sydney*
PRENTICE-HALL OF CANADA, LTD., *Toronto*
PRENTICE-HALL FRANCE, S.A.R.L., *Paris*
PRENTICE-HALL OF JAPAN, INC., *Tokyo*
PRENTICE-HALL DE MEXICO, S.A., *Mexico City*

C

EDITOR'S NOTE

This series offers the depth and richness of the divine message of
salvation proclaimed to us by Christ. The theology, or "faith seeking understanding," contained here is not on a catechetical level,
nor yet on a complex, higher level; it is clear and nontechnical,
but at the same time adult and thorough. It is a scholarly presenta-
tion of revelation.

These volumes do not adopt an apologetic approach. They

neither attempt to justify Catholic faith nor aim at convincing those who do not profess it of the reasonableness of believing. This series is written primarily for those who already believe, who accept the Church as the living continuation of Christ, and the Scriptures as divinely inspired.

The authors do not attempt a philosophy of God or of Christianity, but a study of the mystery of God seen through the eyes of faith. The mystery of faith will not be dispelled by the study of these books. It will remain.

Since some background in philosophy on the part of the reader is needed, and cannot in every case be presumed, there are times when philosophical terms will need to be explained. Philosophical reasoning is very much a part of speculative theology.

Although the breakdown of the series is along traditional lines, each volume is designed to emphasize the oneness of God's plan of salvation and not its different facets. Distinction is made in order to unite. What is taught in the Scriptures is stressed, so that it may be seen how men of the Bible understood the message entrusted to them. The historical aspects of doctrine as held by Christians are then treated: the testimony of the early Christian writers and the liturgy to the belief of the Church; the controversies and heresies that necessitated defense and precise formulation, and finally, the magisterial teaching in each subject area. In this way speculative theology, or the present understanding of each mystery, is not seen in isolation from the sources of faith.

Thus, the revealed Christian message is viewed as the *tradition* (in the fullest and best sense of that theological term) expressed in and through the Church over the centuries—more explicitly formulated, from age to age, and with further applications. But it is still the same saving message begun in the Old Testament and perfected in the mystery and person of Jesus Christ.

One last point is important. Although the study of theology is an exercise of intellect, it can never be exclusively this. The message of Jesus Christ is a living Word, an invitation to participate in the saving event of the redemption, starting in this world by faith and the union of grace, and culminating in heaven by vision and immediate union. This invitation demands response or living faith. The study of the Christian message through theology requires such response, for the message is not something that was heard and assented to once. It is a Word addressed to us that requires our vigorous "Yes" for a lifetime.

CONTENTS

vii

CHAPTER ONE

WHAT THINK YOU OF CHRIST?

"What think you of Christ?"

This is the most important question to be asked or answered by any man. By you. On a man's answer to this short question depends his state of mind and heart during life and after death—he is either with Christ or without him. "How do you evaluate Christ?" would be another way of putting this same question. Do you consider him the most important person in your life, the one in whom your hopes for happiness lie?

I

Many, perhaps most men, do not. Some, even of those who consider themselves Christians, would hesitate to subscribe to the evaluation of Jesus that he is the most important person in human life. He is dead long since, on a cross outside the city walls of old Jerusalem. His ideas were good, uplifting, even surprisingly modern, in some respects. But as a person, is he as important as one's parents or friends or teachers or, above all, oneself? Many do not think so.

The chief contention of this book will be simply this: Jesus Christ is the most important person in human life—in the life of all men and of each man. No one can safely disesteem him; no one may ignore him. To study him is to come to grips with the reality of life.

What do you think of Christ now—at this stage in life? Do you evaluate him exactly as you did during elementary school days or high school years? You have new ideas and new problems as you enter upon adulthood. You no longer accept your parents' or teachers' words simplistically, perhaps not even at face value; you are accustomed to analyze and criticize them in an effort to understand what they are saying and teaching. This should be the case in regard to your faith, too—the faith you profess as a Christian, whether Catholic or not. You are examining your beliefs during these years, to see why you hold them and what it is you really do hold. Such is the normal, natural evolution of the growing mind and heart and soul. This book is intended to help you grow in all your human faculties.

If you call yourself a "Christian" you are named with Christ's name. Likely, you are a churchgoer. Why? Why go to your Christian church to worship God? So many people seem to go merely for social and sociable reasons: to be seen, to wear new clothes, to meet people, to get parents "off your back," to fulfill school rules. It can become mere routine, rite, and rote. But you are a *Christian*. Your church experience is supposed to be a contact with the living Christ, your Lord and Savior, the most important person in your life. . . .

What to think of Christ, then? Was he just a man of his time, limited as any Jew of that century and place would be? Some have termed him a visionary who proclaimed an unreal "brotherhood" that wasn't there and never will be here. For others, Jesus Christ is a wildeyed revolutionary, completely wrong about the ways of man to man. People called "Docetists" claimed that he was a dream that never really happened, in the way of ordinary individuals. "Strong" men have cursed him as weak, a pitiful preacher of spiritual pap called "humility." Weak men have maintained that he was a phony hero, built up by later followers into the impossibly good and great man of the gospels. Charlatan or fool, deluded or deluding, madman or plotter, "nice guy" but hopelessly out of date, out of touch—all this he has been called, and will be called.

2   Or is he very *God*? Could he be divinity itself become human for our sakes—for your sake? The Creed of Nicea says yes, that this is so: "The Son of

God . . . God from God . . . who for the sake of us men and for our *salvation* . . . became man. . . ." (D54)

The world we live in, by and large, says he is not God, not the sovereign Lord of the universe. Its substitutes are a scant improvement. Christ is not God, but something must be ultimate so that we can have a norm to judge by. Cosmic energy? Chance? The power of reason? Humanism? This world, perhaps? Skepticism about this world?

One of these must be supreme, if Christ is not the sacrament of him who is supreme. If men ignore Christ, perhaps he will go away. They would be fools to deny him. This would make him seem important. Just "include him out," in the deathless phrase attributed to Sam Goldwyn. He will be forgotten eventually. He will cease to be.

Shall he die, then? In your life, shall he die? You could allow this to happen. He was a "stumbling-block to the Jews, and foolishness to the gentiles." (1 Cor 1,23) Each of us has a good measure of both Jew and gentile in him in that sense, which tends to weaken faith.

What is your answer to the question with which we began? What *do* you think of Christ? Here and now? At Mass, Catholics repeat some remarkable statements about Christ "You alone are holy . . . You alone are Lord most high. Through him and with him and in him is *all* glory to the Father, in unity of the Holy Spirit . . . Of his kingdom there shall be no end." Catholics believe these things of Christ, the Prince of Peace. "My peace I give to you. . . ." (Pre-communion prayer of the Roman rite)

But is he Prince of Peace in a world blasted by bombs, rife with rumors of war, teetering along the sagging tightrope of diplomatic relations? If Christ is true God, why is our world in such a mess? Sometimes the UN building seems to sound more like a huge soap-box for diabolism than a chamber for the reasonable settlement of international problems. Peace, peace, and there is no peace. Could this be because answers provided by Jesus have failed to answer the real questions of mankind and thereby have failed to fulfill man's needs? Have poverty, disease, sheer hunger disproved his claims to be Prince of Peace? People, indeed whole peoples, are confused often in spite of their good will. They do not know the opportunity or challenge or meaning of life, and meander aimlessly through the sustained inanity called by teachers of morals "the world and its pleasures." In the film *La Dolce Vita,* nameless, faceless creatures keep crying out from a sea of slime: "Why are we doing this? Why?"

It may be that Christ did not give us the answers, and is a pseudo-prince of peace; or that he simply did not know the answers, and is not to blame.

Suppose a man does accept Jesus Christ as God and man. He reads of him in the Scriptures, hears him preached on Sundays, prays to him and through him—as he has always done. More than that, however, he begins to wonder about a number of things. Things like the questions that follow.

Is this "Jesus Christ," who is both God and man for the Christian, one

3

"thing" or two? Is he an individual, in psychology's definition of that word? Is he a divine being or is he a human being; if the latter, is he a human person? Did he and does he have a human personality? If not, then is he truly human? Was he just like us except for sin? If so, how? Did he know everything but never reveal this, acting instead like any Jew of his day? He said he knew not the day nor the hour of the last times. (Mk 13,32) Was he ignorant about other things, too—the way to happiness, for instance, or the truth about life?

If he were truly human was he weak, like us . . . afraid at times . . . unsure? Did he have a truly human, male body, subject to heat and hunger and fatigue, able to reproduce; or was it different, somehow? Were his reactions to people always so right and kind if he could call down woes on Pharisees (Mt 23) and callously let the dead bury their dead (Mt 8,22)? Was he the beloved, humane individual they claim when he used a whip on tradesmen in the Temple (Jn 2,14ff) and cursed a harmless fig tree for not bearing fruit out of season (Mk 11,14)? Was he so kind to his mother when he called her "Woman" when he did speak to her (Jn 2,4; 19,26)? At least there is no recorded occasion when he called her "Mother."

If he were divine, could his so-called human life have been actual in every sense? Was he potentially the best athlete, the greatest scientist, the finest artist who ever lived? How could he say at one time, "I and the Father are one" (Jn 10,30), and later come out with, "The Father is greater than I" (Jn 14,28)? Was he disturbed in mind, perhaps, to voice such schizophrenic statements?

These are some of the questions and problems that may well occur to you at this stage of your life and education. Perhaps you did not have them a while ago, but your desire for an intelligible faith is greater now than ever before, it is safe to assume. You now see some of the difference it makes whether you accept Christ as God or merely as a man. Or as God only, and not as man in the full sense. You see better the need for studying him to find out more about the answer to the crucial question, "What is your opinion about the Messia?" (Mt 22,42), which has come to have reference to no one but Jesus. "What think you of Christ?"

If your answer is to be, "Truly this man was the Son of God," then your life will be different. You cannot ignore him.

This book is meant to help you in learning more about this unique person, in discovering primarily his answers to these questions and problems. The book will not give all these answers, but will assist you in finding them. "Come and see" (Jn 1,39) was the way Jesus himself encouraged inquiry. You ought to feel somewhat like Andrew and Peter on that occasion. They were good men, searchers. But they needed much more knowledge before they could have any certainty about him of whom "Moses in the Law and the Prophets wrote, Jesus the son of Joseph of Nazareth." (Jn 1,45)

4

CHAPTER TWO

CHRIST
IN HIS CHURCH
TODAY

Before examining the actual revelation of Christ found in the Scriptures, we should reflect a bit on the belief in Christ that is ours if we are Catholics. As living members of his body, the Church, we have received God's gift of faith. What are we being taught about this most important person? How is he being presented as the object of our faith? When we go to the revealed sources, we can do so with renewed curiosity as to how this teaching and belief have evolved while remaining substantially the same, if we are first clear on the contemporary teaching of the Church. It is not that we prejudge all matters because of our present belief, then discover explicitly in the sources what we have already decided must be there. This would be childish and a false method. We ought, however, to observe how the Church is witnessing to Christ in our day, and then see how this compares with the sources of belief. Inevitably, the manner of witnessing will be somewhat different now from the apostolic age; also inevitably, it must be essentially the same, for Christ was and is the one final and sufficient revelation of God, "yesterday and today and the same forever." (Heb 13,8)

What do Catholics believe about Jesus at present? Most of the following ideas can be accepted by all Christians, with some minor adaptations. A useful compendium of faith is the Apostles' Creed, which proclaims him,

> the only-begotten Son of God, our Lord, who was conceived of the Holy Spirit, born of the Virgin Mary, suffered under Pontius Pilate, was crucified, died and was buried; he descended into hell; he rose again the third day from the dead, ascended into heaven and sits at the right hand of God the Father Almighty; from there he shall come again to judge the living and the dead. (D6)

The Church gives us this creed and explains its biblical language to us. Jesus, Son of Mary, the Church says, is reigning with God the Father, having won redemption for us by the threefold salvation-event of his passion-resurrection-ascension. This is the essential proclamation about him today, just as it was in the time of Peter and Paul in the early days of the Church. (Cf. Ac 2;3;13;17.) Nowadays, in place of apostles we have bishops proclaiming the *kērygma,* the good news of Christ, and witnessing to the faith handed down intact from his apostles. As Peter and the others preached Christ to the Jews and gentiles, so the Church today preaches this kerygma in Sunday sermons, in special services like Forty Hours, in instruction classes for converts, in missions and weeks of reparation to the Sacred Heart, in radio and television sermons, and all the other occasions for proclaiming that Christ is the true Son of God and Son of Man. Thus do we hear him preached or *proclaimed.*

We also hear him *taught.* The apostles did not only proclaim Christ as the Savior of men but taught converted Christians as well, in order to deepen the faith these had received through preaching. This was the *didachē*—the careful elaboration of the core of the salvation-announcement which eventually became the *euaggélion,* the gospels as we know them today. We too are taught, and our faith is deepened, by the wise words of Christ through his Church. Our bishops teach us by word and example, often through pastoral letters. They meet in synod or council to decide on fitting answers to present-day questions, and solutions for present-day problems. These Christian teachings they pass along to us by word and writing. Above all, the head over all the bishops of Christ, the bishop who sits in Peter's place, on occasion carries

6

on this teaching office for the whole world. The Catholic world takes heed. Ordinarily he teaches through letters addressed to the entire Catholic world— "encyclical" letters. (For the binding force of such encyclicals, cf. *Humani Generis*, 1950, No. 20, NCWC translation.) We shall consider in the following pages the content of a few of them for their Christological teaching.

ENCYCLICALS

Quas Primas

In 1925, Pope Pius XI issued *Quas Primas* ("On the Kingship of Christ") and established the feast of Christ the King in the Roman calendar on the last Sunday of October each year. "The peace of Christ in the kingdom of Christ" was Pius' motto, and this encyclical was one way of attempting to bring about that peace more securely. Only in acknowledgment of the royal dominion of Christ the Prince of Peace would lasting peace come to the world, a world then remembering the horrors of trench-warfare that scarred central Europe for years. The enemy of this peace was the spirit of laicism or secularism, the ignoring of God and his Christ. With Soviet Russia newly formed, the pope reminded the world that attempts to organize human society without reference to God and his rights in this world are equivalent to a denial of him. They can lead only to war, not peace. There seems to have accrued abundant proof of the wisdom of these words in the intervening decades.

Christ is meant by the Father to be king over the minds and hearts of men, so that his gentle words and ways will be the standard of action for all. Worldlings cannot understand and will not accept such a king. They fear him . . . because he is a crucified king. Many are his "hard sayings" to a worldling's ears: obedience, self-control, courage, suffering for the sake of others. An irony of our times is that the great ideological enemy of Christ is now demanding and getting from its followers just these human qualities in the service of anti-Christ. Truly, the devil is the "ape of God."

But the true king is Christ, incarnate God.

> For it is only as man that he may be said to have received from the Father "power and glory and a kingdom" (Dan 7,13–14) since the Word is consubstantial with the Father and has all things in common with Him, and consequently has supreme and absolute dominion over all created things. (America Press translation, No. 9)

St. John saw his name as "king of kings and lord of lords" (Ap 19,16), the natural ruler over men and angels in virtue of the union in him of human nature with a divine person, the eternal Son of God. Acknowledgment of his kingship, then, is our way of fighting the secularist spirit—though the peace we attain may well be through pain and sorrow, as we imitate him who "made

7

peace through the blood of his cross." (Col 1,20) The kingdom is spiritual, and it is a thing of now. Its king, our king, is Jesus Christ.

Miserentissimus

In 1928 the same Pius XI wrote *Miserentissimus* ("On Reparation to the Sacred Heart of Jesus") as a complement to his previous teaching on the kingship of Christ. Devoted reconsecration to Christ the King was the hoped-for result of the 1925 letter, and the wholehearted expiation of sin of this one. The situation of a quarter-century ago seems sadly familiar now:

> Disrespect for the discipline of the Church is on the increase among the faithful, as also disrespect for ancient traditions upon which the Christian life has been built, by which domestic society is governed, by which the sanctity of marriage is protected. The process of educating youth has been weakened or spoiled by too much effeminacy, and even the right to educate children in their religion has been taken away from the Church. Christian modesty is forgotten, sad to say, both in our manner of life and our dress, especially by women. There has come into existence, too, an uncontrollable desire to possess the base things of this world, an unreasonable regard for civil interests, an intemperate searching after popular applause, a despising of legitimate authority and of the Word of God, by all of which the faith itself is shaken to its foundations or placed in jeopardy. (America Press translation, No. 18)

Such reminders breathe the spirit of Christ, the sinless one. All men are urged to accept God's superabundant graces, to make his love abound more than the sin which seems so prevalent. Joining with Christ, victim for sin, Christians can fill up the sufferings of their Lord and bring back to his peaceful kingdom sinners who up to now have been refusing his grace.

> A wondrous bond joins all the faithful in Christ, the same bond which unites the head with the other members of the body, who are the communion of saints, a bond full of mystery which we believe in as Catholics and by virtue of which individuals and nations are not only united to one another but likewise to the head "who is Christ: from whom the whole body, being closely joined and knit together . . . derives its increase to the building up of itself in love." (Eph 4,16) This, too, was the prayer which Jesus . . . at the hour of his death made to his Father. (*Ibid.*, No. 11)

Christ's heart, said Pius, like any human heart, symbolizes that great love.

Lux Veritatis

In 1931, the fifteenth centenary of the ecumenical council of Ephesus in 431, Pope Pius XI issued a commemorative encyclical *Lux Veritatis* ("The

Light of Truth") which contains much of modern Catholic teaching about Christ our Lord. Basing his words on Scripture, as Ephesus had done, he says:

> . . . the Word of God did not unite himself to any individual man already existing; rather, the one selfsame Christ is the Word of God eternally dwelling in the bosom of the Father and also made man at a moment of time. Divinity and humanity are bound together in Jesus Christ, Redeemer of the human race, in the marvelous union which is rightly named "hypostatic" [that is, personal]. Sacred Scripture shows this clearly, for in it the one Christ is not only called God and man, but also is clearly shown acting as God and also as man. He died as man; he rose from the dead as God.
>
> This means that the same One is conceived by the Holy Spirit in the womb of the Virgin, is born and lies in the manger, calls himself the Son of Man, suffers, dies nailed to a cross—and is also the same One who is called by the Eternal Father "My beloved Son. . . ." (Mt 3,17; 17,5) (Cf. NCWC translation, p. 20.)

This personal union of the human nature with the divine Son is necessary for true Christianity. Without it Christ would not truly be God but a mere human like the rest of us, and need redemption himself instead of being able to redeem us.

With this dogma safely held, however, the whole world is different. It is raised to a level even higher than that of the first creation, for,

> among the offspring of Adam there is one, namely Christ, who possesses everlasting and infinite divinity, and whose manhood is united with it in a mysterious and most intimate manner: Christ our brother, possessed of human nature, but also God-with-us, Emmanuel, who by his grace and merits has brought us back to the divine Source of all and recovered for us that heavenly blessedness from which we had fallen away by original sin. Let us therefore be of grateful mind, follow his precepts, imitate his example. In this way we shall be partakers of the divinity. . . . (Ibid., p. 23)

Mystici Corporis

Pius XII continued this praise of Christ in his encyclical *Mystici Corporis* ("On the Mystical Body") in 1943:

> Who is in a higher place than Christ as God, who as the Word of the Eternal Father must be acknowledged to be the "firstborn of every creature"? (Col 1,15) Who has reached more lofty heights than Christ as man, truly born of the immaculate Virgin, yet also the true and natural Son of God . . . ? Who has been so exalted as he, who as the "one mediator of God and men" (1 Tim 2,5) has in a wonderful way linked earth with heaven . . . ? (Cf. Paulist Press translation, No. 37.)

9

As head of the mystical body he gives direction to his members, guiding them by his grace dispensed through the Church which he left behind to carry on his mission. The goal for all is a share in the holiness of God himself, in imitation of the God-man who is the perfect exemplar of all virtues. To this end, Christ continues his sanctifying work through the sacramental life of his body: "It is he who through the Church baptizes, teaches, rules, looses, binds, offers, sacrifices." (*Ibid.*, No. 58) He sends the Holy Spirit to dwell within his members and unite them as God's holy people. Unquestionably he is the most important person in our world, for only in him can we be offered as a pleasing sacrifice to the Father; only in him can we offer our gifts to God.

Mediator Dei

This theme of our sharing in Christ's sacrificial love was amplified in 1947 in another encyclical of Pius XII, *Mediator Dei* ("On the Sacred Liturgy"). Near the beginning of this document, a summary of the earthly life of Jesus contains many of the themes of Christology and will help to unify the data which we shall consider in the Old and New Testaments in later chapters.

> No sooner, in fact, is "the Word made flesh," than he shows himself to the world vested with a priestly office, making to the eternal Father an act of submission which will continue uninterruptedly as long as he lives. . . . He plans his active life among men with no other purpose in view. As a child he is presented to the Lord in the Temple. To the Temple he returns as a grown boy, and often afterwards to instruct the people and to pray. He fasts for forty days before beginning his public ministry. . . . As teacher of the truth, he "enlightens every man." . . . As shepherd he watches over his flock, leads it to life-giving pasture, and lays down a law that none shall wander from his side. . . . At the Last Supper he celebrates a new Pasch with solemn rite and ceremonial, and provides for its continuance through the divine institution of the Eucharist. On the morrow, lifted up between heaven and earth, he offers the saving sacrifice of his life, and pours forth, as it were, from his pierced heart the sacraments destined to impart the treasures of redemption to the souls of men. All this he does with but a single aim: the glory of his Father and man's ever greater sanctification. (NCWC translation, No. 17)

The priestly life of Christ no doubt belongs more to the treatise on the redemption than to this one, but the basic fact that makes the historic redemption possible is the Word made flesh. No consideration of the incarnation may entirely disregard it. Why did God become man? Was it solely that he might do a priestly work of reconciliation, or would it have happened in any case, apart from man's need? For one school of thought within the Church, the followers of Duns Scotus (d. 1308), the more satisfying answer is that God wanted to confer upon mankind the greatest possible gift of his love. He wished to draw man as closely as possible to himself, whether man had sinned or not; the incarnation was God's way of manifesting his infinite love.

For another school, the Thomists (after Aquinas, d. 1274), this is a possible but not an historical answer. Revelation seems to indicate clearly that God sent his Son into the world to redeem the world, which *de facto* needed redemption after universal sin. Pope Pius XII seems to favor this opinion at the very beginning of *Mediator Dei*, when he says:

> Mediator between God and men (1 Tim 2,5) and high priest who has gone before us into heaven, Jesus the Son of God (Heb 4,14) quite clearly had one aim in view when he undertook the mission of mercy which was to endow mankind with the rich blessings of supernatural grace. Sin had disturbed the right relationship between man and his creator; the Son of God would restore it.

Sempiternus Rex

This relationship between the mysteries of incarnation and redemption was further explored and described by the same pope in 1951. On the fifteenth centenary of the council of Chalcedon, he wrote *Sempiternus Rex* ("The Eternal King") to recall the doctrine taught by that great synod in 451. After reprobating some modern errors which have tried to repeat the false ideas condemned at Chalcedon, he says:

> The untold magnificence and merciful character of our redemption is apparent only when one believes with a pure and sincere faith that in Christ there is but one person, the person of the Word, uniting two quite distinct natures, the divine and the human, different in their properties and their operations.
>
> . . . The Word suffered truly in his flesh, shed his blood on the cross and paid to the eternal Father superabundant satisfaction for our sins; from this arises the certain hope of salvation for those who follow Christ with true faith and lively charity. . . . (NCWC translation, Nos. 41,42)

The pope attributes the ancient error of those who did not accept Chalcedon's terms to an "initial misunderstanding in terminology" (No. 33), and suggests that such a misunderstanding should no longer be perpetuated. In accord with the spirit of Christians all over the world today, he invites those who believe as Catholics and as Nestorians to an agreement on the meaning of the terms person and nature; he is sure that once the usage is made clear, unity of doctrine will be indicated immediately.

This is not the case, according to Pope Pius XII, regarding some others who term themselves Christian but refuse to accept the reality of the God-man as Chalcedon states it. "Kenotic" theologians who teach that "in Christ there is a limitation of the divinity of the Word" should be condemned no less than Docetists who limit his humanity, for they "reduce the entire mystery of the incarnation and redemption to lifeless and empty shadow." (No. 34) The basic condemnation of Ephesus was reserved to those whose modern counterparts so exalt the psychological independence of the human mind and will of Christ that they seem to make of his human nature a second "individual," not really united to the Word in the sense of being one person with him. Such a human autonomy cannot be admitted in the God-man. The Son of God remains the only responsible subject of all his acts, whether these stem from his divine mind and will or from his human faculties. (Nos. 35–38)

In the intellectual climate of our own day, such warnings to Christians are much in order. Philosophical terminology is changing, and emphases are no longer the same as at the time of theological definition. Pius XII reminds us that no matter how we use terms, we must adhere with all the faith that is in us to the reality proclaimed by Chalcedon. This is the faith given to us by Christ and his Church, and enunciated in 451:

> The Son [of God] and our Lord Jesus Christ is one . . . perfect both in his divinity and in his humanity, truly God and truly man composed of a body and a rational soul. He is consubstantial with the Father in his divinity, consubstantial with us in his humanity, *like us in every respect except for sin* [cf. Heb 4,15]; he is begotten of the Father in his divinity before time; in this last age for us and for our salvation he was begotten in his humanity of the virgin Mary mother of God. . . . The Lord Jesus Christ is not split or divided into two persons; there is one selfsame, only-begotten Word, God the Son. (D148)

This is the faith of Chalcedon; it is the faith of Catholics, still proclaimed by Chalcedon's champion, the bishop of Rome. In Chapter Eight we shall see the development within the Church in her understanding of Scripture that led to this proclamation of faith; for the moment, we shall simply note with gratitude that the successor of Pope Leo I still teaches the same.

Haurietis Aquas

A most extensive and penetrating papal discussion of the mystery of Christ occurs in Pius XII's 1956 encyclical, *Haurietis Aquas* ("On Devotion to the Sacred Heart of Jesus"). Resuming and repeating the themes of previous popes and his own previous teachings, he develops the central fact of our religion: that God loves each of us with a boundless love, and that Jesus Christ is the divine-human personification of that love. His human, wounded heart is the symbol that reminds us of the redeeming but often rejected love of God for man. This love should draw from us a corresponding love, generous, outgoing, sacrificial.

Such an attitude on our part is necessary, the pope teaches, for otherwise we shall emphasize the wrong things in Christianity, or some one thing that may get out of proportion and spoil the integrity of our faith. Devotion to the heart of Christ as the symbol of his redemptive love is devotion to the incarnate Word which historically proved that love, extending through both testaments and even to the end of time. (NCWC translation, Nos. 28–54) This devotion takes the form of adoration, for

> we know that His Heart, as the noblest part of human nature, is hypostatically united to the person of the Divine Word and must therefore be adored in the same way in which the Church adores the person of the incarnate Son of God. We deal here with an article of Catholic faith since this point was already solemnly defined in the general council of Ephesus [Can. 8; D120] and the second council of Constantinople. [Can. 9; D221] The second reason . . . stems from the fact that His Heart, more than all the rest of the members of His body, is the natural sign and symbol of his boundless love for the human race. (NCWC translation, Nos. 26, 27)

Focusing our attention on the human heart of Christ as the quite understandable symbol of his love for us, we are in no danger of forgetting the reality of the incarnation: that God really did become *human* for our sakes.

> For the Word of God assumed not a fictitious and empty body, as some heretics maintained as early as the first century of the Christian era. . . . [Cf. 2 Jn 7.] But the Word actually united to his divine person an individual, integral and perfect human nature. . . . Nothing, therefore, was lacking in the human nature which the Word of God joined to Himself . . . [which was] in no way diminished or changed in its spiritual and bodily capacities, that is, a nature endowed with intelligence and free will and the rest of the internal and external faculties of perception, sense appetites and all natural impulses. (*Ibid.*, No. 49)

Among these impulses, love is most important and central. In Christ, love is threefold: the infinite love which he has in common with the Father and the Holy Spirit; his own human spiritual love based on his perfect knowledge of God and men; and his human emotional love, based on the affections of his human heart. According to Pius XII this human heart, which in Western usage is symbolic of a man's whole being and life given to another whom he loves, is fittingly considered the focal point of all God's love shown for man in the incarnation of the Redeemer. It symbolizes not merely Christ's emotional love nor merely an isolated act termed "love," but the entire inner life of the Savior, formed and informed by those most perfect infinite and finite loves which are found uniquely in him. Devotion to his sacred heart, then, ensures our adherence to the faith of Chalcedon and of the apostles. It is devotion to God, and to God-made-man for love of us. (No. 103)

The emphasis in this way of approaching Christ is an appreciation of God's great love for us, shown in the gift of his Son as our redeemer. Such 13 appreciation is absolutely basic to Christianity, is indeed the central matter in our religious practice. Devotion to the loving heart of Christ results in a loving service of God, as we attempt to give back to him some measure of the gifts with which he first endowed us. Such loving service can be a perfect way of living our faith. It expresses a generous form of that love of God and neighbor which marks those who have learned from Christ.

The vicar of Christ in 1956 thought it well to remind us of this.

CHURCH LIFE TODAY

Pope John XXIII continues to preach and teach the same loving Christ by word and example. The faith of Christians is the same today as it was in Peter's time. We are taught not only by the *kērygma* and *didachē,* but also and perhaps more effectively in the worship of Christ by Christians, for here we come into personal contact with this second person in God, and cannot but learn of him. The sacraments are more and more being considered in theology to be personal acts of Christ directed toward our personal sanctification and more vital participation in the life of his body, the Church. In holy communion we consume Christ, the bread of life, the one bread in which we are all united as grains to make up the whole. In the other sacraments we encounter this same Christ extending to us the particular graces we need and seek.

In the Western custom of reserving the blessed Sacrament from one eucharistic celebration to the next we find the Son of God incarnate showing us the mystery of our faith. Tabernacle and altar center our eyes and attention; the sanctuary lamp silently announces his presence in our midst. Reverent genuflections proclaim without words that we adore him as our divine high priest. The veils of women, the tipped hats of men, heads bowed in passing a church, all bear public witness to this faith that is ours in Christ's redemptive role. The open doors of the house of God welcome many each day, if only for a brief visit to remind ourselves that we are at one with Christ in his will to save us. He has come from heaven and in the realm of sacrament at least he is ever present with us. He has tabernacled among us, as did Yahweh with Israel of old. He stays in our midst, both in the eucharist and above all in becoming one with us in his Church.

The central devotion of Catholics is to the Mass, and Sunday is the great day of its celebration. Through this sacramental rite we keep Christ central in our lives. The cycle of seasons in the liturgical year keeps Christ contemporary with us, as we relive with him the wonderful events of our redemption through him. The proper parts of the Mass for the various times and feasts of the Church year will richly repay study. We will be able to pray them devoutly on the next occasion of celebration. During Advent we repeat the ardent cries of Israel for a redeemer; at Christmas we welcome that Savior born again in the action of the Mass. During Lent we endure with him the growing opposition of this world; during Passiontide we, like fainthearted apostles, try to understand his way of saving the world by suffering and death. Easter brings us the glad gospel cry: He is risen! Pentecost assures us again of his holy Spirit's presence among us to give life to our world under the protecting hand of God.

In so many ways, then, Christ still preaches and teaches and gives us example, through the temporal extension of his incarnation that is his Church. The modern Church is the new chosen people, designated by baptism instead of circumcision, wandering at times in a desert of uncertainty that includes the threat of total destruction for the whole human race, but directed securely by the new Moses, Jesus Christ. He, unlike Moses, has not stopped short of the promised land. He has pressed on and entered once and for all into the heavenly holy of holies. He will lead his faithful followers there, if they but remain faithful to him.

This is our faith. By it we live; in it we hope to die.

CHAPTER THREE

CHRIST
IN THE CONTEXT
OF HIS TIME

In moving from a consideration of Jesus Christ as we encounter him in a Church of twentieth-century men and women to the son of Mary portrayed in the New Testament, we necessarily traverse the time-space continuum too quickly. At first we find ourselves somewhat out of our element. First-century Palestine, a tinderbox corner of the Roman Empire which even today is rife with plots and riots, is the cultural background of the gospel story. We will assume that the reader has a general idea of its history.

THE TWO TESTAMENTS

The relationship between the Old Testament and the New Testament has been a fascinating subject of study ever since the latter was formulated. No final explanation is ever likely to be given because of the essential mystery involved. Christ used Old Testament personages and events to illustrate his teachings, indeed as the necessary substrate of his teachings. The apostles delved deep into the Scriptures in their eagerness to show their fellow countrymen that the Nazarene was truly the fulfillment of Israel's hopes. All Christians hold that God's revealed word through Moses and the other Old Testament writers foreshadowed the reality to come, that it was the "pedagogue" leading men to the great Teacher, the rabbi who never attended the schools but who showed wisdom such as no man has ever shown before or since. The exact relation between the two testaments, however, remains a problem and a mystery. Two opinions relevant to this difficult question are worth mentioning in broad outline.

The first would suppose that God from eternity planned the history of his chosen people with the earthly life of Jesus in mind, so that his supernatural interventions were meant originally to be types or prefigures of our Lord, valuable chiefly for the light they would throw on him at a later time. The second opinion would hold that Christ at his own discretion and with complete freedom adapted his teachings and actions to Israel's sacred history as occasion offered. Theologically, a combination of the two explanations is desirable and even necessary. The history of the chosen people is a salvation-history, initiated and carried out by the merciful God. His plan is a unified one, which begins in the strict sense with the creation of man. It reaches the onset of its climax in the birth of the Savior in Bethlehem, David's city. He who is born there is the fullness of Israel. It is equally certain that Jesus and the New Testament writers looked to their Scriptures (the inspired writers mainly employed the Septuagint, the Greek translation of the Old Testament) for apt comparisons and telling images. They were selective in so doing; they had to be.

Take the idea of kingship, for example. As a king, Solomon was no doubt more splendid than David his father, but Solomon's brand of kingship contained some details best omitted from any picture of ideal kingship. So did David's, but at least his story included contrition and the attribution to him of Psalm 50[51], the magnificent *Miserere*. For the Jews, David and not Solomon was the perfect example of God's anointed one ("meshia"); their salvation was to come from David's family.

Another example of New Testament adaptation of an Old Testament passage would be Psalm 117[118] as it appears in Mk 11,10. In the Old Testament, it is a fervent, dramatic prayer of thanksgiving to the Lord, who is the savior of Israel from enemies who had surrounded her. The psalmist comes to the Temple and cries: "Open to me the gates of justice. . . . The stone which the builders rejected has become the cornerstone. By the Lord has this been done; it is wonderful in our eyes." The priests at the gates sing out: "Blessed is he who comes in the name of the Lord; we bless you from the house of the Lord. The Lord is God, and he has given us light. Join in procession with leafy boughs up to the horns [corners] of the altar." The psalmist responds: "You are my God, and I give thanks to you. . . ."

Undoubtedly the "stone" refers to Israel. The image is transferred to Christ in New Testament preaching to the Jews. (Ac 4,11) Did God inspire the psalmist so that his song could be used by Peter later, or did he inspire Peter to use this familiar feast-day acclamation as a most fitting way to show his fellow countrymen how Jesus fulfilled their Scripture?

The case is similar to the "procession with leafy boughs." Does this reference occur in the Old Testament primarily because God had foreseen the procession with palms and the outcries in praise of Jesus? Surely he intended from eternity that the use of this psalm by those who welcomed Jesus to Jerusalem would illustrate the harmony of his revelation, and so he made available a thanksgiving prayer most suitable for the occasion. Many Christians still avail themselves of both gestures and words, bowing down and praying in conjunction with the threefold acclamation of Is 6, "Holy, holy, holy, Lord God of hosts," the snatch from Psalm 117[118]: "Blessed is he who comes in the name of the Lord!" Catholics use this prayer at the *Sanctus* of the Mass.

The truth about the proper relationship of the two testaments probably lies somewhere in a combination of the two opinions outlined above. The fact is that we simply cannot understand Jesus Christ except in the context of his time and place, his religion and culture. Before we meet him in the New Testament directly we must attempt some description of these, lest he seem unreal to us because divorced from his context.

OLD TESTAMENT WITNESS

Israel's God

First of all, Jesus was born a Jew. He belonged to a nation which had long preserved strict monotheism as its most precious religious possession. Indeed, it was the reason for its existence as a nation. "Hear, O Israel! The Lord is God, he alone!" (Dt 6,4) This prayer, the *Shema*, has been for centuries the morning and evening prayer of Jews, the expression of their experience of Yahweh, the Lord. Faith in this unique God had made them a people, a chosen people since Abraham's time. The covenant of circumcision (Gn 17,1–14) promised them the blessings of a permanent dwelling in a homeland of their own, with the Lord as their only God. The covenant of Sinai which was made in Moses' time (Ex 19–20) reaffirmed this agreement, after the Lord had proved his loving care by freeing them from slavery in Egypt.

The first commandment expressed his will for them. "I, the Lord, am your God, who brought you out of the land of Egypt, that place of slavery. You shall not have other gods besides me." (Ex 20,2f) Through long centuries of struggle with themselves and against other nations, the Israelites came at last out of their sixth-century exile in Babylon back to Jerusalem, to live the monotheism they had been taught. Their devotion to the one God had crystallized during fifty years of absence from the holy city. Made firmer still by the next five centuries of siege-living in Jerusalem (from 538 B.C. onward), the identification of "peoplehood" with true monotheistic faith was one of the greatest obstacles Jesus faced. It was also the chief reason for his method: gradual revelation of the role that was his in the work of salvation, in Old Testament terms, until hearts were ready for the grace of *Christian* faith. The strength of Jewish monotheism, however, proved to be a weakness, in the sense that the light of rabbinic commitment to it made it difficult for Jesus' contemporaries to see.

Soteriological Expectation

How could this be, when we see so clearly—or think we do—that the entire Old Testament heralds the coming of the Messia, points him out with unmistakable evidence? Let us recall that no exact correlation of texts and events in the two testaments may legitimately be constructed, as if the story of Israel was always clearly the story of Christ-as-he-was-to-come, and as if the Jews of his day read their own history in that way. The references to him we now gather into chapters such as this one are scattered through a large collection of books, many of which were unavailable to the people. They knew the Scriptures as their teachers shared them with them—piecemeal. In addition, false Messias had arisen and would arise. Jesus to some of his contemporaries appeared to be just one more prophet or holy man. His task was to show the reality of the difference. For this, he could build on Israel's expectation of a savior sent from Yahweh, someone through whom the Lord's salvation would come.

This soteriological expectation was very real in Israel; by the time of Jesus the people hoped ardently for a savior. Ever since their experience in the Exodus they had believed firmly in God's special providence for them. "Thus says the Lord: Israel is my son, my firstborn." (Ex 4,22) They hoped for salvation at Yahweh's hands. The prophets' great refrain was: the Lord will intervene to save us. At first this hope of theirs was a general one concerned with political freedom, moral perfection, and earthly satisfaction of a high order for the people in the promised land. It concerned a *thing* rather than a person. After the establishment of the monarchy (c. 1050 B.C.) as Yahweh's means of exercising dominion over his people, the salvific expectation took on the characteristic of religious loyalty to the reigning king. The dynasty was *19* thought to be the chosen instrument of Israel's salvation.

David

The king *par excellence* for Israel was David. This charismatic representative of Yahweh who came after Saul and the judges was the personification of the nation Israel: wise, strong, religious-minded in spite of his faults. David enjoyed the protection of Yahweh against his enemies. He entered into a covenant which would ensure an eternal dynasty blessed by God, which in turn would carry out Israel's obligation toward Yahweh. (2 Sam 7) The Father-son relationship was extended from the people as a whole (Os 11,1) to this king, and memorialized in various psalms.

> The Lord said to me, "You are my son; this day I have begotten you. Ask of me and I will give you the nations for an inheritance and the end of the earth for your possession." (Ps 2,7–8) The Lord said to my lord, "Sit at my right hand, till I make your enemies your footstool." (Ps 109[110]1)

Each successive king was in turn to be the sign of Yahweh's favor; not even major sin in them could destroy the dynasty's place in God's salvific plan for his people.

But gradually the kings grew weak politically and morally, until finally the two kingdoms disappeared entirely under the foot of the alien conqueror. Israel's hopes were transferred from a present to a future king, to a "new David" who would naturally be a Bethlehemite (Mich 5,1), a Prince of Peace with the gifts of the Spirit of Yahweh upon him. (Is 11,1–3) This perfect king in the image of David was to come on the Day of Yahweh, when God would intervene for the last time to save his people.

> Therefore the Lord himself will give you this sign: a virgin [Heb.: young woman] shall be with child, and bear a son, and shall name him Emmanuel, God is with us. (Is 7,14) For a child is born to us, a son is given to us; upon his shoulder dominion rests. They name him Wonder-Counselor, God-Hero, Father-Forever, Prince of Peace. (Is 9,5)

The dominion of this mysterious scion is vast and forever peaceful; he will rule from David's throne over a kingdom which he confirms and sustains by judgment and justice, both now and forever. (Is 9,5–6; cf. Jer 23,1–6; Ez 17,22–24; 34,23–24) Although this saving king was to be Yahweh's instrument, his kingdom was not necessarily coextensive with that of Yahweh in Israel's earliest expectation. This came later, when the people identified their time of salvation with Yahweh's final intervention, which would make Israel the leader of all nations in a universal kingdom of God at the end of time.

Messianic Hope

This latter type of hope seems to have become common in Israel around the time of the Babylonian exile (587–538) and after, when they were re-building the Temple in Jerusalem. The Day of Yahweh would be the end-time, and the new David would re-establish God's kingdom in this final period of the world's history. The deeds of this ideal king became part of the vision of the future, as in Zacharia 9,9–11:

Rejoice heartily, O daughter Sion,
    shout for joy, O daughter Jerusalem!
See, your king shall come to you;
    a just savior is he,
Meek, and riding on an ass,
    on a colt, the foal of an ass. . . .
The warrior's bow shall be banished,
    and he shall proclaim peace to the nations.
His dominion shall be from sea to sea,
    and from the River [Euphrates] to the ends of the earth.
As for you, for the blood of your covenant with me,
    I will bring forth your prisoners from the dungeon [of exile].

Such passages became the foundation for the technical use of the term "Messia" during the intertestamental period: the Anointed of Yahweh, who was to restore the glory of his people Israel. Unfortunately, in the minds of many the religious aspects of this coming kingdom became dim or were lost. Expectation was centered almost entirely on material gains, to be won when their God should intervene to save them from their present misery under the Greeks or Romans or Herod's motley line.

The kingdom of Yahweh, as the prophets proclaimed it, was to be primarily the will of the Lord realized in mankind, with a consequent re-birth of mankind and the whole world. The Hebrews well knew that only Yahweh could accomplish this, and they believed that he would do so in his own good time. This event they tried to hasten, however, by their continual prayers for succor. Too often they asked for earthly goods only, but in such case they mistook the reality. The kingdom was in fact to be the final and universal realization of the will of the Lord. The people did not know how this was to be accomplished. Certainly they had no faintest idea that Yahweh would come himself in human form to do it. This notion they would have dismissed as an unthinkable paradox: *"God is not man,* that he should speak falsely, *nor human,* that he should change his mind."* (Num 23,19)

They clung to their belief that he would intervene somehow, through a Jewish king whom they came to call the Messia, God's Anointed. This was all they expected, but it was already very much.

Suffering Servant

Two other themes of salvation were available to the Jews in their holy Books, although these do not seem ever to have been integrated into their expectation of a kingly Messia. One is that of the Suffering Servant in the four songs of Deutero-Isaia. (42,1–4; 49,1–7; 50,4–9; 52,13–53,12) The Servant may be a particular historical figure or a personification of Israel; in either case, Christian writers from the beginning have applied the prophecies to Christ, taking the lead from the Master himself as the gospels report him. (Mk 8,31; 9,30; 10,33f; Lk 24,26)

> I will make you a light to the nations, that my salvation may reach to the ends of the earth. Thus says the Lord, the redeemer and the Holy One of Israel, to the one despised, whom the nations abhor, the slave of rulers: When kings see you, they shall stand up, and princes shall prostrate themselves because of the Lord who is faithful, the Holy One of Israel who has chosen you. (Is 49,6f) He was spurned and avoided by men, a man of suffering, accustomed to infirmity, one of those from whom men hide their faces, spurned, and we held him in no esteem. Yet it was our infirmities that he bore, our sufferings that he endured. . . . But he was pierced for our offenses, crushed for our sins; upon him was the chastisement that makes us whole, by his stripes we were healed. We had all gone astray like sheep, each following his own way; but the Lord laid upon him the guilt of us all. . . . Like a lamb led to the slaughter or a sheep before the shearers, he was silent and opened not his mouth. . . . Because of his affliction he shall see the light in fullness of days. Through his suffering, my servant shall justify many, and their guilt he shall bear. (Is 53,3–7.11)[1]

That Yahweh would bring salvation to Israel by the atoning death of an Israelite or of the nation rather than by that of brute animals is original in the book of Isaia; it is to be found only here in the entire Old Testament. Surely the idea did not take hold of the popular mind. In fact in Jesus' day the rabbis were attributing the bitter punishments of the servant songs to Israel's enemies rather than to Israel itself. Jesus' method of teaching the necessity of suffering shows clearly how little the ordinary Jews could countenance any type of salvation other than a glorious one in which their God would manifest himself in power for the sake of his people.

Son of Man

The other somewhat neglected salvation-theme is found in the book of Daniel, which saw,

---

[1] A period between verse numbers indicates that the verses cited are successive but nonconsecutive.

> One like a son of man coming,
>   on the clouds of heaven;
> When he reached the Ancient One
>   and was presented before him,
> He received dominion, glory and kingship;
>   nations and peoples of every language serve him.
> His dominion is an everlasting dominion
>   that shall not be taken away,
> His kingship shall not be destroyed.
>
> (Dan 7,13f)

This "one like a son of man" is generally agreed by exegetes to be a personification of the Jewish people, so that the vision describes Israel's triumph and exaltation as ruler of the nations in the times of the ideal king. "Son of man" at first meant merely an individual human being, a man; with the passage of the years of Israel's longing for deliverance, it came to have overtones of expectation not entirely clear to us now, but surely derived from this vision in the second-century book of Daniel. It did not mean "Messia" directly in our Lord's time, for he used the phrase "Son of Man" frequently to indicate himself, while continually enjoining silence on his disciples concerning his messiaship. From his usage, it is evident he meant the phrase to serve as a convenient transition-concept toward a belief in him as more than mere man. An intertestamental book, the *Similitudes of Henoch,* speaks of "the son of man" as an apocalyptic, transcendental figure unlike anyone in this world. Quite possibly such usage indicates that the title connoted in Jesus' time a kind of superman who would found the final kingdom of God on earth in the "last days" of the world. If so, Jesus' use of it to describe himself takes on added meaning for us now.

The Covenant

These monotheistic Jews, then, were eagerly awaiting an intervention of their God and Father on their behalf. For them, *Torah,* the Instruction (later, "the Law,") was their God-given way of life. Obedience to it was their means of keeping their side of the covenant and of assuring the Lord's fulfillment of his promises to them. In their loyalty to the Law and the prophets lay their infallible means of pleasing Yahweh and of retaining their favored status as his special people.

God's Name

Another aspect of the filial attitude of pious Jews toward Yahweh was their reverence for his holy name. In Semitic thought, the name expressed the real nature of a person or thing; it was equivalent to the existing reality so named. Thus, God's name YHWH, the sacred "tetragrammaton" first revealed to Moses on Sinai (Ex 3,14), stood for Yahweh himself in all his awesome presence. In Jesus' day it could be pronounced only by the high priest in his official capacity in the Temple, where God's presence was manifested by the *shekinah,* the mysterious luminosity thought to shine in the holy of holies. The Jews adopted other titles for Yahweh: the Holy One of Israel (Is 1,4; 47,4; Ez 39,7); the Almighty (Est 13,9), Savior (Is 43,3; 45,15; Os 13,4; Sir 51,1); King (Jer 10,10); the Most High (Dan 4,31); the Blessed One (Mk 14,61); or very commonly, *Adonai* (Ex 6,3), my Lord. (The Greek translation of the Old Testament known as the Septuagint regularly used the word *Kyrios* to translate *Adonai,* so that "the Lord," whether in Greek or Hebrew, was the ordinary way of speaking of Yahweh in Christ's time: Dt 3,24; Jud 16,16; Jer 32,17.) This was the one only God, the God of Abraham, Isaac, and Jacob, the God of their fathers and forever; no other was God besides him. (Is 42,8)

Lord (Kyrios)

Even a cursory glance at the book of Psalms will demonstrate quickly how thoroughly the title "Lord" was identified by the praying Israelites with their God. The two names are used in conjunction frequently, in testimony to their unwillingness to pronounce Yahweh, and for the same Holy One in different verses of the same psalm. (Cf. Pss 3,8; 4,2.4; references could be multiplied throughout the Psalter, Isaia, and Jeremia, as well as the other books of the Old Testament.) The usage "Lord God" is seen in Zachary's *Benedictus* (Lk 1,68) and Mary's *Magnificat* (Lk 1,46f), both of which reflect prevailing Jewish custom in prayer.

The Temple

The Temple of Jerusalem has been mentioned as the site of God's unique presence among his people, the place from which his "glory" shone forth in token of his continued favor. The Temple was really another aspect of Israel's monotheism, for in the exclusiveness of Temple worship was guarded the exclusiveness of their religion. Just as no other gods were allowed besides Yahweh, so only in the Temple was his name invoked, for here only was his presence experienced fully. In the book of the wisdom of Jesus Ben Sira (Ecclesiasticus), a lengthy description is given of the wonderful ceremonies in the Temple on the Day of Atonement. From it we gain some idea of the majesty of the cult of Yahweh familiar to the Jews of Jesus' time, some sense of the awe they felt at the sight of the high priest conducting the service.

> How splendid he was as he appeared from the Tent,
> as he came from within the veil!
> Like a star shining among the clouds,
> like the full moon at the holyday season; . . .

Vested in his magnificent robes,
    and wearing his garments of splendor,
As he ascended the glorious altar
    and lent majesty to the court of the sanctuary.
When he received the sundered victims from the priests
    while he stood before the sacrificial wood,
His brethren ringed about him like a garland,
    like a stand of cedars on Lebanon;

*   *   *

With the offerings to the Lord in their hands,
    in the presence of the whole assembly of Israel.

*   *   *

Then all the people with one accord
    would quickly fall prostrate to the ground
In adoration before the Most High,
    before the Holy One of Israel.

Then hymns would re-echo,
    and over the throng sweet strains of praise resound.
All the people of the land would shout for joy,
    praying to the Merciful One,
As the high priest completed the services at the altar
    by presenting to God the sacrifice due;
Then coming down he would raise his hands
    over all the congregation of Israel.
The blessing of the Lord would be upon his lips,
    the name of the Lord would be his glory.
Then again the people would lie prostrate
    to receive from him the blessing of the Most High.
            (Sir 50,5f. 11f.17–21)

The Temple then was identified in the people's minds with their nation and their religion. God's name was proclaimed there because he was there as the protecting Father of Israel, the glory of his people.

SUMMARY

These themes of Old Testament religion all served to prepare the way for the coming of Jesus the Christ, not by a rigid one-to-one relation of prophecy to fulfillment or type to reality, but by a general relationship which gradually focused upon the son of Mary as the one who fulfilled perfectly all the aims and desires of Israel. We are not justified in lining up the so-called messianic texts of the Old Testament on one side of a page with the corresponding New Testament texts on the other and saying, "Lo, here . . . lo, there he is!" Old Testament messianism is simply not identical in character with that of the New Testament which fulfilled it. Various themes of the former testament which seemed disparate and even contradictory—e.g., glorious king and suffering servant—find their reconciliation in the one Lord Jesus. But this we know only after the fact. Before the fact, no Jew had the slightest suspicion that it could ever be. At best, the themes seemed parallel lines unconnected. It is our perspective of faith which enables us to see that they joined at the horizon: Christ.

Perhaps the best figurative way in which to conceive this matter is to make Jesus the center of many radii, all pointing from the encircling history of Israel in toward him. The Temple, the holy name, the covenant in blood, Moses, Abraham, Emmanuel, David, the Law on stone and in the hearts of men, the paschal lamb, Adam, Daniel's "son of man," the serpent raised in the desert, God the shepherd of Israel, manna, the suffering servant, the anointed king, wisdom forming the world, the glory of God in pillar and cloud, the savior to come, the "Son of God," the creative word—all these themes and historical events of the Old Testament can now be seen as pointing eventually to Jesus of Nazareth. He is the fullness of Israel. In him are summed up all the hopes and desires of his people. Conversely, the New Testament is simply unintelligible except in this context of Old Testament religion.

TRUE MESSIANISM

We must never forget, however, that Christ in fulfilling these hopes transformed them. Messianism is therefore not an apologetic concept but a theological one. It is based on biblical evidence to be sure, but is suffused with the later clarity of realized history. In the Old Testament the radii seem at times to have different centers, or to proceed outward to an uncertain periphery. Only in Christ do they come together and find their centering. To reveal the pattern of these radii took Jesus' lifetime, as we shall see in the following chapters. For now, we should try to put on the mind and heart of Israel for a while, as we hear her crying out for salvation in words employed in the Advent liturgy:

> Come, Lord, and do not delay; show us thy face. O shepherd of Israel, hearken . . . rouse your power and come to save us. O Lord of hosts, restore us; if your face shine upon us, then we shall be safe. (Ps 79[80]2–4) Your ways, O Lord, make known to me; teach me your paths. Guide me in your truth and teach me, for you are God my savior, and for you I wait all the day. (Ps 24[25]4–5) A voice cries out: In the desert prepare the way of the Lord! Make straight in the wasteland a highway for our God! Every valley shall be filled in, every mountain and hill shall be made low. . . . Then the glory of the Lord shall be revealed, and all mankind shall see it together; for the mouth of the Lord has spoken. (Is 40,3–5)

The Baptist

The above imagery is Oriental, picturing the preparation for the coming of a great king. John the Baptist, in the authentic Jewish tradition, came up out of the desert crying this same message, hailing the advent of "one mightier than I." This one would proclaim himself to be the "way." (Jn 14,6) Later, the tradition of approaching the Father through him would become known as "the way." (Ac 19,23)

The Baptist is the link between the two testaments, the last and greatest of the prophets pointing directly to Christ. He gave testimony to the light which shone in the darkness of each man and of all men. The Baptist still bears witness to us, for his story is told in the Sunday gospels of Advent each year. There he reminds us that true "change of heart" is necessary if we are to recognize our savior coming anew to us in the Christ-mass. Each day, too, we hear his accents in the pre-communion prayer adapted from his word of proclamation: "Behold the Lamb of God, behold him who takes away the sins of the world!" (Jn 1,29) The paschal lamb saved Israel from the final plague; Christ our Pasch is sacrificed for us (1 Cor 5,7), still taking away the darkness of our sins and enlightening us, as the Baptist foretold.

Mary

If the Baptist is the link, Mary is the material out of which the Mediator of the new covenant is formed. By God's wise providence she was made ready to be his mother. Little do we know of the details of her life—mainly that she was *there,* created by God to bring his Son into the world of Israel through a daughter of Israel. Perhaps she was of David's royal line; if she was not, at least her husband was. Matthew 1,1–16 testifies to the Davidic lineage of Joseph, the just, virginal husband of Mary the virgin. She is born under the Law, and her son's blood is entirely Semite. (Gal 4,4) His physical characteristics are derived from her. Artists try to picture her son, each according to his time and people. Only one thing do we know about Jesus' earthly appearance: he is a Jew, and resembles Mary.

She is his mother . . . mother of the Savior. This is her great privilege, the basis for all her greatness and the only reason for her importance. Christian piety has fulfilled her own prediction as we find it in Luke (1,48), for all generations have called her blessed. She is blessed for the reason she so humbly gave: he that is mighty has done great things for her. All her holiness, all her privileges are due to God's gracious gift. Conceived without sin, she owed the first grace-filled moment of her life to the future merits of her Son. She, like us, is nothing apart from Christ—but God's plan has established a once-for-all connection between these two, mother and son, for the salvation of the world. He sent his son not as a full-grown man into the world but "born of a woman" (Gal 4,4); and the woman's name is Mary. For her motherhood we love her. She gave fulfillment to Israel through her faith-filled commitment to God's holy will. Hers was the most perfect act of trust ever prayed by a human being: "Be it done unto me according to your word." (Lk 1,38) Thus she begins her role as mother of God's son, as the instrument of the recreative Word. She is, in Coventry Patmore's phrase, "our only savior from an abstract Christ."

Much of the antagonism to Catholic veneration of Mary—when it is not a justified reaction against excessive claims or pseudo-piety—seems to stem from a failure to accept the biblical revelation about her and her son in all its truth. Christ for many Christians seems to remain abstract, a shadowy exemplar of that "spirit of brotherhood" which makes a man a Christian. Well-meaning as such an idea of Christianity may be, it is absolutely divorced from the truth. The Christ we love and try to imitate is no abstraction, no mere symbol of "the American way." He is the Word made flesh, made as human as any of us.

The incarnate Word hungered and grew tired and had to wash his feet after walking the dusty roads of Palestine. He experienced the passion of anger. He was born of a human mother whom his heavenly Father chose from the women of all time. His Father prepared this mother as no other could be prepared, all with a view to her role in the redemptive plan. The privileges given her of initial grace, of virgin motherhood, of sinless behavior were all given as directed to the mission of her son. They were privileges of grace, not of earthly glory.

Mary should not be an obstacle, then, to understanding and cooperation among Christians. Far from this, she should be for all who profess faith in Christ what she was for her own day: the human but God-given proof that his son did truly become man, that we have been saved by one of our race, that Israel's hopes have been fulfilled in an Israelite, according to the promise. (Gn 22,18; 26,4)

CHAPTER FOUR

CHRIST
IN ST. MARK

You believe in Jesus Christ. Can you imagine the state of mind of those who first lived with him and gradually came to accept the man from Nazareth as identified with the great God himself? Imagine the shock they must have had, the violent change in thinking that was entailed in this. The majestic God of Israel is so intimately present to this carpenter, Mary's son, that there is a sense in which he too is to be called "God." (Rom 9,5; Jn 1,1;

Jn 1,18; 20,28; 1 Jn 5,20; Ti 2,13) We believers seldom experience any such change in our ways of thought; we are almost born with our faith, a gift from God through our parents. Even those who accept the faith as his gift after adulthood seldom go through a complete overthrow of their religious ideas when they accept Christ. Imagine if you can the condition of the first disciples whose monotheism was the central fact of their religious lives. "Hear, O Israel, Yahweh is your God, He alone," was their daily prayer. (Dt 6,4) These men were to be challenged to accept a fellow Jew as their Lord. They were to conceive of him and worship him in terms of the only God. What task more difficult could be given to anyone than that of believing in Jesus Christ as Israel was asked to believe in him?

Perhaps you do not really believe in Jesus Christ. Maybe you do but wonder why you believe, or what your belief really means when you have not tested it by scientific or other adult standards. Are you sure that Christ is the Son of God? Imagine the frame of mind of rabbi Saul as he subpoenaed Christians and dashed off toward Damascus to throw more of them into jail. Saul became the new man Paul when the risen Christ appeared to him and showed him the truth about himself. Why and how did Saul change? The New Testament tells that story; to it, we listen.

A Problem

But what are we listening to when we hear this New Testament read out? How reliable a record is it of events so important and portentous? Surely those who wrote it were not disinterested, objective narrators; they were men intimately involved and committed to the Jesus of whom they wrote. They were not reporters on the scene recording what he said and did, and the re-actions of others to him, in the manner of modern journalists. The New Testament is a *post factum* account, highly colored by the devotion of its writers to this man and his memory. Does not this render the record suspect, and us suspicious of its truth?

Toward an Answer

We do not have the time here, nor is there need, to attempt a lengthy disquisition on the reliability of the gospel accounts, or their special nature as religious or salvation-history, that is, history permeated with God's purpose to save men in his own way. The New Testament is God's inspired word just as truly as the Old Testament is; it continues the same story. The New Testament brings the story to fulfillment as it tells of the return to the merciful God of wayward children who have lost the pathway to heaven. This return is in and through Christ.

The New Testament is the Christian record of Christ, guaranteed from error by the wise God but told in the words and accents of first-century Jews who have come to believe in Jesus as the Messia, very Lord and God. The writers recounted the events from the memory of the primitive Church, but individual and collective memory was long in those days—much longer than ours. They were remembering the most important things of their lives: the words and deeds of one who lived as no other man, who spoke as no other man, who did deeds which no man had ever done—above all, who had deliberately died on a cross for their sakes, and had appeared to many afterward to show that he was truly raised up by God. The first Christians spoke their memories of him, preached them, exchanged them, controlled one another's recollections by their own, eventually wrote the four accounts which we call gospels, as well as the Acts of the Apostles (a book of community history), various epistles (twenty-one in all, bearing the names of five apostolic personages), and the Apocalypse. They died for their belief that these accounts were true, and that the man from Nazareth was indeed the Son of God. Surely their witness is reliable. We are safe in affirming that much. Whether their faith was true faith is another matter, but of the reliability of their witness as such there can be no historical question.

Many an erroneous thinker has died for his beliefs. The importance of the witness of the apostles lies in the *substance of the beliefs* they died for. The great question for us is whether their faith corresponds to supernatural reality, but in the New Testament we certainly possess the record of their faith.

These accounts are not in the form of a romance about a wonder-working leader whose every word is inspiring, whose every deed marks him out a hero. The Christ of the gospels presents many problems for the believer, even in the unvarnished and matter-of-fact style of the evangelists. If the authors had wished to glamorize him, if they were letting their own personal faith distort all that they wrote of him, then surely they would not have included such passages as "The Father is greater than I." (Jn 14,28) . . . "Why call me good? One is good, God." (Mk 10,18) . . . "Not my will, but yours be done." (Lk 22,42) . . . "My God, my God, why have you forsaken me?" (Mk 15,34) . . . "He could do no wonderful works there, because of their lack of faith." (Mk 6,5f)

Do not such words cast doubt on any claim that in him we are in contact with God himself? Is he not saying that he is not conscious of being one with God, that he knew he was not God? Interesting item, this. The documents which are the basis of our faith and were written to deepen our faith include these passages. Could it be that the early Christians who put these documents together had no fear of any adverse effect from the inclusion of such items, but rather thought it necessary for the complete picture of this man whom they worshipped together with God their Father? It could be, we say, limiting our argument for the moment.

In reading the gospels we should approach them with open minds to find what is in them and evaluate it objectively and faithfully. We are not much interested, in the present treatment, in developing any "proof" that Jesus Christ is true God and true man; we are concerned with theology, not with apologetics, and theology examines what is already known with the certainty of faith. But we do want to attempt a deeper penetration into the meaning of the Scriptures so that our faith will be deepened and our wisdom increased. We shall try to achieve this penetration in more than one way.

Gradual Revelation

The first way consists in using the gospel according to St. Mark, which is the basic gospel. In it we shall witness the gradual revelation which Jesus made of himself, and the gradual growth in faith in him which the disciples experienced. This should enable us to realize better the revolution in religion that is contained in our familiar expression: Jesus Christ, true God and true man. Sometimes we forget one or other aspect of the truth, that he is truly God and truly man.

In Mark's gospel we are in touch with Jesus as the primitive tradition spoke of him. We can discern fairly well the method of the Master through the method of Mark. Scholars are agreed that this account is less personal, less theologically developed, than the other gospels—that it is quite near to the ideas of Jesus as he expressed them and reflects a tradition drawn from Jesus' life that had undergone little amplification in the intervening decades. Reflecting as it does the deepest convictions of the Markan community of early Christians, probably at Rome, it is worthy of belief. This gospel is inspired by the Spirit of God, who used the Roman community and St. Mark as instruments of committing this gospel to the entire Church. Let the exegetes conclude which incidents and words come from which sources; they have a perfect right to make the attempt, and we rely on them for their conclusions. The insights that increased biblical knowledge gives the living Church are one of her treasures. We come to this gospel, then, with both the desire to know, and faith. We shall seek Jesus Christ, and we shall find him.

MARK'S GOSPEL

"The beginning of the gospel of Jesus Christ, the Son of God." (Mk 1,1) Mark leaves no doubt of his own belief, in this first sentence, or rather this title, of his accounts. His faith has already been made secure by the Spirit's coming. Here he addresses himself to the task of showing how he and others came to post-Paschal belief. They did not come easily, as all the accounts make clear. The strict monotheism nurtured in the people for many centuries and purified by their temptations and failings precluded their accepting as God anyone but the majestic Lord (Yahweh) whose name was unutterable. His nature was inimitable, his works of power boundless. The men of Israel had no image of this true God. He was invisible and transcendent. An image would have been an idol. He was the One who is, who makes everything else exist but is not beholden to any of his creatures. For a mortal to claim his

Name was to blaspheme, and thus to be worthy of death. The prophets had been great and were his spokesmen, but they were not to be confused with God. The kings were great and exercised power for him, but they were his subjects only. Only one was God: the Lord. This was the faith of Israel. It was the faith of those with whom this Jesus lived and spoke and worked.

Mark's salvation-history begins not with the birth and youth of Christ, but with the preaching of John the Baptist. The "mightier one than he" came to be baptized. Thus began the gradual revelation of who and what Jesus was, to be climaxed on Calvary and perfected on Pentecost. Mark's gospel does not extend to the latter event but ends by describing Jesus exalted to heaven at the right hand of the Father, a Semitic way of saying that he is equal to God. In between, we read the good news of his coming.

Divisions

For reasons of space limitation we must summarize the data of Mark's gospel rather than expand them at length. For the sake of clarity, we may divide the gospel into two main parts, the first dealing with the Galilean ministry (chs. 1–10) and the second concerning Jerusalem (chs. 11–16). The first section is climaxed with Peter's confession of faith in Jesus as Messia (8,29; hereafter all citations shall apply to Mark except as otherwise indicated); the second seems directed to Christ's profession before the high priest that he is the Son of the Blessed One. (14,62) The incidents related as occurring before and immediately after these two events serve to prepare the disciples for them, and to illustrate their deep meaning.

FIRST SECTION   In the Galilean period, the gospel relates how Jesus drew disciples to himself by his teaching, and by the divine power he showed in working miracles of healing and exorcising. We can learn much about his problem and his method by noticing the reaction of those around him. They by no means accepted him immediately as anything more than a prophet or emissary of God. "They were astonished at his teaching, for he was teaching them as one having authority, and not as the scribes." (1,22) After he drove out the unclean spirit, "they were all amazed, so that they inquired among themselves, saying 'What is this? What new doctrine is this? For with authority he commands even the unclean spirits, and they obey him!'" People kept coming to him from all over as a result of hearing the rumors about his wondrous powers over disease, even leprosy.

In Chapter 2, Mark relates two telling incidents: the cure of the paralytic, which he uses to show Jesus' power to forgive sins, and the defense by the Master of his disciples' plucking wheat on the Sabbath, to show that he is lord of the Sabbath. After the first, "they were all amazed, and glorified God, saying, 'Never did we see the like.'" No reaction is recorded after the second but the same theme is presented again in the beginning of Chapter 3, where on the Sabbath he cures a man with a withered hand and is from then on the object of the pharisees' deadly enmity. They attribute his powers to his being in league with Satan (3,22), for they well know that these powers and claims cannot stem from humanness alone. Their solution, however, is to embrace darkness rather than the light. This Jesus calls the sin against the Holy Spirit of God. (3,29)

Jesus meanwhile selects twelve "to be with him"; these will later be the apostles, his willing witnesses to the ends of the earth, but now they are just getting to know him. He instructs them by word and work, leading them into the mystery of his coming and his person. They have no doubt about his true humanity; his mother and his relatives are all about them. But is he any more than human? They hear him teaching in parables, and they later press him to explain these parables to them in private. They see and hear him in the storm at sea; their response to his power over the elements is expressed in wondering amazement: "Who, then, is this, that even the wind and the sea obey him?" (4,40) They know of the demoniacs' cries (3,11; 5,7) which call him "son of the most high God." Three of the twelve accompany him to the raising of Jairus's daughter from death. After they recover from their astonishment (5,42) they appreciate the thoughtfulness of his asking the bystanders to give her something to eat. They all accompany him to Nazareth, where his townsmen reject him as being but an artisan, "the son of Mary." This, incidentally, is the only time that Mark mentions our Lady or that the New Testament gives him this title. (6,3) "And he could not work any miracle there, beyond curing a few sick people. . . . And he marvelled because of their unbelief." Surely the disciples must have wondered even more than he did at his inability to convert and convince his own kindred. They were learning the truth about him that to accept him is to change one's whole way of thinking and living. It means trying to be like him as he is like the Father.

Two marvelous works occur before their eyes, without their understanding either them or him. Feeding five thousand men with five loaves and walking calmly on the windblown waves were not yet enough to make them see with the eyes of their hearts. Numerous kindly cures struck them, however. Finally the "Ephpheta" spoken to the deaf and dumb man elicited the cry: "He has done all things well. He has made both the deaf to hear and the dumb to speak." (7,37) They are ready to be challenged by him after another multiplication of bread.

> "Though you have eyes do you not see, and though you have ears do you not hear? . . . When I broke the seven loaves among four thousand, how many large baskets of fragments did you take up?" They said, "Seven." And he said to them, "How is it that you do not yet understand?" (8,18ff)

He cures a blind man gradually. Mark seems surely to intend some symbolic application to the disciples' blindness toward Christ, for he inserts this incident just before the climactic declaration of Peter.

Messianic Secret. Before we consider this climax, we may well reflect a little on one paradox in his method of teaching: the reiterated command not to tell others of his wonderful words and works. This is called "the messianic secret" of Jesus, and is explained variously. Perhaps it was merely his fear of letting his reputation as a wonder-worker get out of hand; crowds are notably unreliable when acting as crowds. These simple people had been long oppressed and could easily become convinced that here was their glorious earthly king, come as Yahweh's instrument to drive the Romans from their land. The irony of the title on the cross would then be Sophoclean. The title "King of the Jews" for which he died on a political charge was the very title he had always rejected.

A more plausible explanation of this messianic secret is that Mark simply reproduces Jesus' own way of gradual revelation of the truth about himself. For the monotheistic apostles to come from initial curiosity about this Nazarene to personal faith in him as Lord—that is, as identified with the God of the Old Testament—for this to take place, circumstances demanded a slow pace and careful guidance. An immediate revelation of the complete truth would have been too much for them.

Like the parents of Samson (Jgs 13,22), they would have expected to fall down and die once they had looked upon the face of God. They would either have had to reject him and leave his company, or, beside themselves with joy, would have been unable even to hear human words bringing the message of God's sacrificial love for men. Whatever the explanation, Mark indicates that the messianic secret is part of the divine pedagogy, and leads to the incident which he now relates.

First Climax. On the way to Caesarea Philippi he asks them who people are saying he is, and they relay the rumors to him: John the Baptist, Elia, one of the prophets. Then, "But who do *you* say that I am?" Peter answers him, "You are the Christ." (8,29) So different from the pharisees' reaction! This is a great moment in the history of God's salvation-plan for men. Peter, in the name of all the disciples, declares Jesus of Nazareth to be the Anointed of God, the Messia, that King long promised to redeem Israel and fulfill her hopes. This is the first and necessary step to be taken toward full acknowledgment of who and what he is. Insufficient in itself as we now know, it still marks a tremendous gain in faith on the part of these disciples.

The Cross. From now on Jesus can reveal the truth about himself more and more. Mark's account makes this quite clear, for he immediately has this Christ speak of his future sufferings, death, and resurrection, and the need of the disciples to follow him along this road of the holy cross. (8,31.34) This is the rub: to follow the true King of Israel will mean taking up a cross for oneself in imitation of him. Peter does not like the idea, and is classed by Jesus with the pharisees on the side of Satan . . . so far from complete understanding is he even now. His ideas need purification.

Building on their messianic faith, Christ gently draws the disciples on to the further identification of him with the Suffering Servant of the Lord. He shows them himself transfigured (9,1ff), and as at his baptism, a voice proclaims his divine sonship. On the way down the mountain he cautions them to say nothing of this until he has risen from the dead. They are baffled, and are not helped by his repeating that as Son of Man he will suffer much and be despised, betrayed, and killed. Even when he reminds them that he will rise on the third day they are not enlightened. "They did not understand the saying, and were afraid to ask him." (9,31) No doubt they were, like us, afraid they *did* understand it, and that he meant what he said. Their earth-bound ideas of God's kingdom had to be raised from thoughts of this world's glory to the true glory of God, even if they had to be raised on crosses. Jesus acts out his instructions. Childlikeness (9,35; 10,13ff), simplicity of belief (9,22f), kindness for his name's sake (9,40), keeping the commandments, and following him in poverty (10,19.21)—all these are the qualities of a man of the kingdom, a man who truly understands what it means to say to Jesus, "You are the Christ."

Again he forewarns them, as they head for Jerusalem: "The Son of Man will be betrayed . . . and they will scourge him and put him to death; and on the third day he will rise again." (10,33f) James and John think they can join him in suffering as also in glory; he accepts them for the role of suffering, leaving the second to be worked out as God has decided. He can guarantee them suffering for his sake, for he will first suffer for them. "The Son of Man has not come to be served but to serve, and to give his life as a ransom for many." (10,45) Mark here has Jesus join the glorious messianic figure of Daniel's prophecy (Dan 7) with the suffering servant of Isaia (chs. 52f) in a distinctive statement of his unselfish sacrifice for the sake of all men. This thought serves as a transition-theme from the first section of this gospel to the second, where we find Christ fulfilling his own prophecy and giving his life for love of us.

SECOND SECTION   Believing still that he is only the Christ, they never ask him how *God* can die. They surely are afraid that what he means to have happen to him is death. Yet Mark at the beginning of Chapter 11 has Jesus telling two disciples to say that "the Lord" has need of the colt that they are to find in the village; "Lord" could mean anything from "sir" to "Yahweh" himself, but in context here it seems to indicate that Christ is now revealing himself as never before. The palm-strewn procession connotes the same idea, as does his driving the sellers from the Temple. One greater than the Temple is here, and is ready to take possession of his kingdom. The crowd is astonished at his teaching once more. The chief priests are enraged and afraid, and they seek to destroy him. He knows them well; he knows their intent. He tells the parable of the wicked vinedressers who killed the "beloved son" of the owner. (12,6) They do not miss his meaning, but have to spare his life momentarily for fear of the crowd.

They challenge him in various ways, with questions of tribute to Caesar and of marriage to several wives; he embarrasses these learned ones before the listeners with his answers and challenges them in turn as to their interpretation of Psalm 109[110],1. The Christ cannot be David's son, for that king in his psalm had called him "Lord"; he must therefore be even greater than David the king.

The people liked to hear him speak thus, of course. Probably the apostles were coming to suspect that he was claiming more than Messia status. They ask him about the end of the Temple and the "sign when all these things will begin to come to pass." (13,4) He describes the future event in apocalyptic terms, reteaching them the now-familiar lesson: "You will be hated by all for my name's sake; but he who has persevered to the end will be saved." He claims to be the touchstone of their religious life, the most important fact of their faith. He goes on to speak of his Parousia, his second Presence, when "they will see the Son of Man coming upon clouds with great power and majesty." (13,26) When will this be? "No one knows, neither the angels in heaven, nor the Son, but the Father only." (13,32) Despite his disclaimer of this knowledge, he is deliberately leading them to see that he is the Son of God in a special sense, different from even the angels in being beloved by God. Even so, there is no sign that they yet understand.

Second Climax.   Mark's story rushes to its climax now. The Passover meal is prepared; during it Jesus institutes the eucharist, giving in food and drink his body and blood as the sign of the new covenant, a sacrifice-covenant with all men. (14,24) What thoughts must have filled their minds and what love possessed their hearts at this first sacrament-meal. But Mark says nothing of this. They go out toward Gethsemani with protestations of their fidelity until death, but they cannot keep awake an hour to pray with him. He prays in all humanness, troubled and afraid of the imminent passion; yet as always, "not what I will, but what you will." (14,36) We are surest of the true humanity of Jesus at times like this, for we too have prayed and been afraid. Truly this is the son of Mary, human like us!

Christ is seized by the rabble directed by Judas, whose name is remembered forever as a curse and a shame. "Then all his disciples left him and fled." (14,50) This, then, is their final human comment on him and his meaning to them: flight from him when the cross becomes clear. Had they truly believed in him before? No doubt they did, but in an all too human way, it seems. They speak brave words; their deeds are not so brave. They leave him to his captors, who hustle him away to Caiphas' where he is to make his own great declaration of his identity before the Sanhedrin and the priests.

> Then the high priest, standing up in their midst, asked Jesus, saying, "Do you make no answer to the things that these men prefer against you?" But he kept silence, and made no answer. Again the high priest began to ask him, and said to him, "Are you the Christ, the Son of the Blessed One?" And Jesus said to him, "I am. And you shall see the Son

37

of Man sitting at the right hand of the Power and coming with the clouds of heaven." (14,60–62)

Mark obviously means this scene to be central to the second section of his gospel. Jesus stands before the official representatives of the Law and proclaims his equality with Yahweh. Perhaps he even uses a form of the sacred Name in saying, "I am." In any case, he accepts the title Son of the Blessed One and foretells his future exaltation and return on terms of equality with the omnipotent God. Well does Caiphas understand his claim, even though he rejects it as impossible. He makes a holy show of indignation at the "blasphemy," the claim to be equal to God. "And they all condemned him as liable to death." (14,64)

Claiming to be the Messia, the Son of God in some way other than by nature, was not a crime punishable by death. The Sanhedrin well knew the affirmation they were condemning him for, and what majesty he had claimed. After his repeated refusals to allow others to proclaim even his messianic character and after his forbidding the apostles to tell all they knew of him, here before the chief priests and elders of Israel near the Temple of his Father he fearlessly declares the truth for his people to hear: I am what you say. You shall see me risen and elevated to equality with Yahweh, and coming in glory to take over my kingdom. They know what he means, and they condemn him so as to prove that he is neither Christ nor beloved Son of God. Later, the apostles will preach the resurrection-ascension as God's direct reversal of this unjust judgment.

But now, Mark only adds the story of Peter's denials, foretold by Christ but none the less shocking in one who has talked so boldly and claimed to love so much. "I do not know this man. . . ." (14,71) The shadow of the cross has darkened even his manly loyalty to Jesus of Nazareth, "this man." No more than that, now; not even "the Christ." But Peter remembered Jesus' words foretelling his falls, and "began to weep." Mark says nothing of Judas after the betrayal; Judas, apparently, did not weep.

Pilate asks him about being "king of the Jews," and Jesus equivalently accepts the title. He is accused of "many things," though Mark does not specify any others, and Pilate seems in Mark merely to yield to the scandalized crowd's reiterated cries, "Crucify him." Ironically, the charge affixed to his cross was only: "The King of the Jews," according to Mark. The Son of the Blessed One dies to save the world, but publicly he is condemned by the state as a political seditionist.

For Mark, such crucifixion between thieves is a fulfillment of Isaia's prophecy (Is 53,12). This is the Suffering Servant of Yahweh, the beloved Son of God.

The mockery of the rabble shows that many remembered his prediction about rebuilding the Temple in three days, and also that he had healed and resuscitated others. "Let the Christ, the King of Israel, come down now from the cross, that we may see and believe." (15,32) This is all they ask, after putting him on this cross because they had refused to see. They would believe neither his words nor his works. They had seen him give sight to blind eyes, but they blinded the eyes of their own minds to him.

Christ Crucified.   On the cross, Jesus shows the completeness of his humanity; he has nails driven through his hands and feet. He suffers the desolation that must be plumbed to the depths to make him break out with the psalmist's prayer, "My God, my God, why have you forsaken me?" (Ps 21[22],2) He cries out with a loud voice, and dies. And at this moment of his story, Mark relates how the Roman centurion, a gentile, in wonder and awe at such a man and such a death, exclaims, "Truly this man was the Son of God." (15,39) Just what the rough soldier meant by this phrase is beyond our knowing, but Mark's meaning is clear: Israel has rejected Jesus . . . his disciples have almost all fled him . . . but here is a simple man from the gentile world to acknowledge this Jesus as "Son of God." Together with the Christ's own declaration before the Sanhedrin, this is Mark's witness to the reality of Jesus, Son of the Blessed One, Son of God. His gospel began with the latter title. Now he ends his story of the mortal life of Jesus with it. His meaning is clear.

He says nothing of the apostles' state of mind; to them, after Calvary, obviously very little was clear.

Christ Risen.   In Chapter 16, which seems to be largely a harmony of things drawn from other gospels, the apostles are "mourning and weeping," and refuse to believe the stories of his rising from the dead. The women who saw the empty tomb "said nothing to anyone, for they were afraid." These are not people primed to believe; they all seem to be doubting Thomases. When finally he appeared to the Eleven, "he upbraided them for their lack of faith and hardness of heart, in that they had not believed those who had seen him after he had risen." (16,14) Mark does not explicitly record their reaction to this severe rebuke, but the obvious inference is that at last they do come to see and believe. This would be necessary if they are to "go into the whole world and preach the gospel to every creature," a gospel by which men shall be saved or condemned, and which shall be accompanied by wondrous signs reminiscent of his own great works.

Mark's final comment on this Jesus is a Semitic profession of divine faith, putting the ascended Nazarene on the plane of Yahweh himself as Lord equal in power. (16,19) It is as Lord that he works with the apostles in their preaching, confirming their words by works which are the signs of their preaching.

Thus far, St. Mark's gospel.

REFLECTIONS   A few reflections on this salvation-history will help focus our attention on its main points. Mark has shown us a gradual change in the apostles' idea of Jesus, from simple wonder through astonishment to   *39* fear, and then acknowledgment that he is truly the Anointed King, the

Messia. Warned of the suffering in store for him, and of its necessity for themselves if they follow him, they cannot believe that Israel's king would reach glory through death. Therefore they fail him at the crucial moment.

His resurrection brings hope with it. So does the command to go out and preach his gospel everywhere, for he is the Lord who sits at the right hand of the Father, exalted to heaven as equal to Yahweh and able to guarantee their preaching on earth by his wonderful works. This, then, is the gospel of the "Son of God."

Is the Jesus of Mark's gospel truly human? No one could doubt it. He grows angry at hardness of heart, shows indignation as well as compassion, disappointment along with gratitude. He admits to no knowledge of the day of his Parousia; he asks information in the various situations of ordinary life. He is obviously a Jew of his time, limited as his fellow Jews are.

But he is by no means only this. Mark's gospel may be termed a careful explanation of how Jesus of Nazareth gradually revealed the ultimate truth about himself. By the time of its composition the title "Lord" was the ordinary way of expressing the divinity of Christ, but this title is saved until the very end of the account for the risen and glorious Christ whom the Christian community venerated. During his mortal life, Mark puts in Jesus' mouth the unusual title, "Son of Man" (Cf. Dan 7,13); this probably reproduces the practice of Jesus, who seems not to have liked the title "Christ" because of its connotations of a merely earthly king. When Peter finally professed him to be the anointed Messia, the King of Israel, Jesus immediately joined the "Son of Man" title with Isaia's picture of the suffering servant so that the apostles would not mistake his kingdom for a merely nationalist one. Even so, they failed to understand. It took the resurrection and his personal appearance to them to change them from unbelief to complete commitment to him as Lord. But once so committed and strengthened by help from him on high, they went out to convert the world, secure in their Paschal faith in the crucified Lord. This is the message of Mark.

CHAPTER FIVE

CHRIST IN ST. LUKE
AND ST. MATTHEW

Now that we have seen the way one gospel recounts the story of Jesus and have tried to understand his impact upon those with whom he lived, we can more profitably go to the rest of the New Testament to confirm our findings and belief. Again we must be selective, leaving complete treatment of the biblical evidence for other times—in fact, for lifetimes. We Christians can never afford to stop studying our Lord in his written word, for this gives base and vitality to our faith, richness to our public worship, meaning to our lives.

LUKE'S GOSPEL

This study of ours could be initiated no better than with St. Luke's prologue:

> Inasmuch as many have undertaken to draw up a narrative concerning the things that have been fulfilled among us, even as they who from the beginning were eyewitnesses and ministers of the word have handed them down to us, I also have determined, after following up all things carefully from the very first, to write for you, most excellent Theophilus, an orderly account, that you may understand the certainty of the words in which you have been instructed. (Lk 1,1–4)

Very probably Luke possessed Mark's gospel as one of these narratives, at least in an early form. In any case, he has much material in common with Mark. We shall concentrate mostly on evidence that he adds to Mark's, so that we may come to understand better the truth of the faith in which we have been instructed.

Infancy

The infancy narrative is the first and obvious addition to the Markan account; the ultimate source for it must be our Lady herself.

> The Lord is with you. . . . You shall call his name Jesus. He shall be great, and shall be called the Son of the Most High; and the Lord God will give him the throne of David his father, and he shall be king over the house of Jacob forever. . . . The Holy Spirit shall come upon you and the power of the Most High shall overshadow you; therefore the Holy One to be born shall be called the Son of God. (1,28.31f.35)

Surely Mary, who had prayed over the Scriptures with the help of special graces from her youth, is portrayed by Luke as having an intimation that her child would be more than a human Messia. To be a virgin mother by the power of the Spirit of God, to bring forth the Holy One, Son of the Most High—surely she was given the grace to know something of who this child was. The words of the account can be understood as indicating only "Messia." But Luke has Elizabeth presently addressing Mary as "mother of my Lord" (1,43), a title for him that Mary immediately uses in her *Magnificat* to praise Yahweh, the saving God of Israel. Zachary, too, identifies Yahweh as the "Lord God of Israel." (1,68) Luke, it would seem then, is using these first two chapters as a commentary on Mark's "beginning of the gospel of Jesus Christ, Son of God." This account reflects the firm religious belief of the third evangelist. Mark and Matthew use the title "Lord" in this most sublime religious sense only at the very end of their accounts (except in Mt 12,8 when, according to many exegetes it bears the meaning "master" of the sabbath). Luke inserts it at once, and favors it throughout his gospel. "Jesus is Lord" is one of the most primitive Christian creeds. (Cf. Ac 10,36.) Luke seems to imply that the first one to sense this was his mother.

The Bethlehem story has the particularly Lukan overtones of universal salvation accomplished in this son of Mary.

> I bring you good news of great joy which shall be to all the people;
> for today in the town of David a Savior has been born to you, who is
> Christ the Lord. (2,10f)

The humanness of this child cannot be doubted without denying this gospel. He is the "firstborn" of the virgin mother, whose intention of virginity seems indicated by her reaction to the angelic message. Since the turn of the century, the virgin birth has been made a test of orthodoxy in certain Protestant theological circles, largely because of the belief that only thus would the true divinity of Jesus be preserved. Certain it is that some of the Fathers of the Church so argued. Such a tradition presupposes that Jesus is the Son of God. Although the viginity of this mother is a supreme privilege corroborating her child's divinity, it is a freely given honor, not a precondition of divine maternity. Revelation tells us this is the way the Son of God took human flesh.

The charming story of the loss of the boy Jesus on the occasion of a pilgrimage feast at Jerusalem, of his being found in the Temple, and the puzzlement of Joseph and Mary at his words, "my Father's business" has the ring of simple truth about it. It is markedly different from the wild imaginings of the apocryphal gospels about the boyhood of Jesus. In domestic obedience at Nazareth he lives the ordinary life of a Jewish boy and young man, preparing for the great manifestation of obedience that will mark his mature period: obedience unto death. By this obedience he merits his name so laden with significance: Jesus, "Yahweh saves."

Familiar Themes

With Chapter 3 Luke reaches the same general material about Jesus that we have seen in Mark: the Baptist, the baptism, Galilean ministry, journey to Jerusalem and the climactic events there. In his second book, *Acts of the Apostles,* he continues the account into the life and times of the early Church, showing how the apostles preached as "Lord and Christ, this Jesus whom you crucified." (2,36) Luke, disciple and companion of Paul, echoes his master in terming Christ "Lord," that is, as sharing Yahweh's dominion over all things. But in his gospel, like Mark, he shows the gradual development of faith in those who saw and heard the Master.

The familiar themes are here. "You are my beloved Son, in whom I am well pleased." (3,22) "I know who you are, the Holy One of God." (4,34)

43

"And amazement came upon all, and they discussed it with one another, saying, 'What is this word? For with authority he commands the unclean spirits, and they come out.'" (4,36) "And devils came forth from many, crying out and saying, 'You are the Son of God.' And he rebuked them, and did not permit them to speak, because they knew that he was the Christ." (4,41) "The Son of Man is lord even of the Sabbath." (6,5) "And all the crowd were trying to touch him, for power went forth from him and healed all." (6,19)

New Material

But suddenly something new is added: "Blessed are you poor. . . . Blessed shall you be when men hate you . . . because of the Son of Man. . . . But I say to you who are listening: Love your enemies, do good to those who hate you." (6,20.22.27) Jesus makes himself the center of religious life, the standard of righteousness, the model of godliness as opposed to the false ideas of sinners. Mercy, forgiveness of others, good works stemming from goodness—these are the criteria of his disciples. "But why do you call me, 'Lord, Lord,' and not practice the things that I say?" (6,46) Luke uses the title here with divine significance. The complaint is as valid today as it was when first uttered.

The "Journey Narrative" occupies Chapters 9 through 18 in Luke, and is special to him: ". . . he steadfastly set his face to go to Jerusalem." (9,51) Everything that Jesus says and does is directed toward the Holy City, the center of God's people, the place of his Temple where his presence is manifested. Many lessons are taught in this long section: detachment from earthly ties (9,62), kindness to those in need no matter who they are (10,33ff), trust in God. (12,22ff) The love of this city which is so dear to his heart breaks out from him in "Jerusalem, Jerusalem, you who kill the prophets. . . . How often would I have gathered your children together, as a hen gathers her young under her wings, but you would not have it!" (13,34) Jesus knows us so well: the rush to be first at table, the lame excuses to avoid anything inconvenient, the prodigal composing his little speech from his pigsty perch while the older son complains about the honor shown the returning wayward, the proud pharisee in the front of the Temple with the humble publican justified in the back. Surely Jesus, like us in all things except for sin and sinfulness, knows us inside out.

Through this section sounds the refrain: "The Son of Man must suffer many things, and be rejected . . . be put to death, and on the third day rise again." (9,22) Luke stresses this even more than Mark, with the corollary for those who learn his lesson: self-denial, the daily cross, consequent salvation. Luke strongly stresses this salvation-theme, and is the only evangelist explicitly to call Jesus "Savior." (2,11) The journey to Jerusalem is a salvation-journey, bringing salvation to Zachaeus the publican (19,10) and all of the house of Israel who would receive him . . . really to all men. But Luke tells us that even the apostles were slow to believe and said to him, "Increase

44

our faith." (17,5) He did, but in his own way and time. His coming passion, which he predicted, was at that moment far from their thoughts of what the kingdom must be. "They understood none of these things and this saying was hidden from them. . . ." (18,34)

Climaxes

Just as Luke tells the incident of Peter's confession somewhat differently from Mark, having Simon confess, "You are the Christ *of God*," so he reports the climactic story of Jesus before the Sanhedrin with a slight variation but with the same meaning.

> "If you are the Christ, tell us." And he said to them, "If I tell you, you will not believe me; and if I question you, you will not answer me, or let me go. But henceforth, the Son of Man will be seated at the right hand of the Power of God." And they all said, "Are you, then, the Son of God?" He answered, "You yourselves say that I am." (22,66–70)

In accepting their understanding of his words, Jesus clearly claims to be what they accuse him of claiming: the Son of God, in the sense of being on a plane with God. For this they engineer his death, although the civil charge is sedition and the title on the cross merely, "This is the King of the Jews." (23,38) Pilate cared nothing for "blasphemy" as a civil charge.

Emmaus

We are indebted to Luke for one of the most informative incidents of the New Testament in regard to the gradual growth of divine faith in the disciples of the Lord. He relates the state of mind of two disciples who "gave up" on Jesus. They were walking toward Emmaus, a town about seven miles from Jerusalem, and talking of the shattering events of the past days. A man came up alongside and asked why they looked so sad. They told him about it,

> . . . concerning Jesus of Nazareth, who was a prophet, mighty in work and word before God and all the people; and how our chief priests and rulers delivered him up to be sentenced to death, and crucified him. But we were hoping that it was he who should redeem Israel. (24,19–21)

This, then, was still the sum of his effect on them. He was a *prophet* blessed by God; they had hoped he was the savior. But at Calvary their hopes had been dashed. So little had they, good men that they were, understood the lesson of the kingdom.

Once more Jesus asked them: " 'Did not the Christ have to suffer these things before entering into his glory?' And beginning then with Moses and   *45* with all the prophets, he interpreted to them in all the Scriptures the things referring to himself." Their hearts burned within them as they listened to his words. Apparently they came to understand the meaning of the Scriptures, but not that Christ himself was speaking to them, for only afterward did they recognize him "in the breaking of the bread." They hurry back to Jerusalem to rejoin the apostolic community, now secure in their Paschal faith that "The Lord has risen indeed. . . ." (24,34) Much like us, they reached intellectual assent to his Lordship when the Word of God was explained to them, but "recognized" him only in the ritual action of the meal, the explanation of God's Word in act.

Risen Christ

Luke has more on the risen life of Christ than Mark has, and emphasizes his kindness to the apostles. His miracles in this gospel are often illustrations of his humaneness and humanity rather than displays of power. In the risen life that same thoughtfulness is shown in his reassurances to them that it is really he.

> "See my hands and feet, that it is I myself. Feel me and see; for a spirit does not have flesh and bones, as you see I have." But as they still disbelieved and marvelled for joy, he said, "Have you anything here to eat?" And they offered him a piece of broiled fish and a honeycomb. (24,39–42)

This is the risen Christ now in glory, the Christ who won Paul's heart on the Damascus road by appearing to him, the Christ now hailed as "Lord" by the Christian community—eating fish with them to show them that in this banquet of the "end-time" his humanness and his resurrected life are not at odds. "Then he opened their minds, that they might understand the Scriptures" about his sufferings and rising; he told them to wait in Jerusalem, "until you are clothed with power from on high." Luke in his gospel account of the ascension juxtaposes two things: "He was carried up to heaven," and "They worshipped him. . . ." (24,51–52) Surely this juxtaposition is not accidental. Luke's account of the same event in Ac 1,9ff does not make this connection. The gospel ends, then, with this act of divine faith on their part, and their return to that holy city and its Temple which had been the goal of Jesus' journeying on earth.

Luke would later write of his gospel, "In the former book . . . I spoke of all that Jesus did and taught from the beginning until the day on which he was taken up, after he had given commandments through the Holy Spirit to the apostles whom he had chosen." (Ac 1,1–2) The Spirit is now to be his strength within them, to make them witnesses to him "to the ends of the earth," as their Easter faith in his Lordship comes to full flower after Pentecost. They preach and teach "the Lord Jesus" now. (Ac 1,21; 2,36) So much have they changed; they will die for him this time.

MATTHEW'S GOSPEL

The third synoptic gospel, St. Matthew's, contains the basic outline of Jesus' life as we have seen it in Mark and Luke: baptism, Galilean ministry, journey to Jerusalem, ministry there, passion and resurrection. The "good news" is the same, though directed to a Palestinian audience: Jesus of Nazareth is the divine teacher who has fulfilled Israel's hopes, but so differently from what Israel had expected that he was rejected by his own people. As a consequence, God's plan for the salvation of the world is to be carried out by the new Israel, the Church founded by Jesus. Written for Jews of Palestine primarily, this gospel stresses the Messia idea from the beginning: "The book of the origin of Jesus Christ, the Son of David, the son of Abraham." (Mt 1,1) How different from Mark's introduction, or Luke's. The theme could be put this way: God is with us, "Emmanuel," in this child (1,23) and in the man who promised at the end of his earthly life, "I am with you all days." (28,20) The story of the virgin birth indicates the providential fulfillment of Isaia's prophecy. (Is 7,14) Matthew loves to indicate such connections, and does so at least twelve times in his gospel. For him, Jesus is simultaneously the end of the Old Testament, that is, its goal, and the founder of the New Covenant in his blood shed for all men. (26,28)

Discourses

The six long discourses of Jesus distinguish this gospel as one of words rather than of works. He is the "prophet from Nazareth of Galilee." (21,11.46) But the works are there, and they work redemption. His miracles show his power over creatures, as also his victory over Satan. Matthew calls him "Lord" only once, and then only in speaking of his risen life. (28,6) Others use the title of him—the centurion (8,6–8), the blind men. (9,28; 20,30ff) But in Matthew's own usage, he is primarily "the Son of Man" and "Jesus." Both titles pertain to his suffering and death. Jesus challenges his followers to face the same trials for him, calling them "blessed" if they will only do so. (5,11–12) He has come not to destroy but to fulfill the Law and the prophets (5,17), but that fulfillment includes his giving, as a new Moses, a new code of life to men: the beatitudes. This he does not as one merely commissioned to promulgate God's will, but as a lawgiver in his own right. "You have heard that it was said to the ancients, 'You shall not commit adultery.' *But I say to you* that anyone who so much as looks with lust at a woman has already committed adultery with her in his heart." (5,27–28) Again and again he lays down the law in these terms: *"I say to you."* God was with them again, teaching them, directing them, in even fuller measure than in Moses' day.

Unique Sonship

Jesus was claiming to be the Son of God in a special way. In a passage unique for the synoptics, he expressed his consciousness of his utter unity

47

with his Father: "All things have been delivered to me by my Father; and no one knows the Son except the Father; nor does anyone know the Father except the Son, and him to whom the Son chooses to reveal him." (11,27) From the parallelism of the saying, we realize that he was claiming a knowledge of his Father equal to the Father's knowledge of him, which of course was infinite. For him so to claim complete knowledge of God was to claim a mind able to contain infinite knowledge; such a mind can belong only to God himself. Moreover, Jesus says that only he can reveal this Father to men. He must be speaking of possessing a supernatural knowledge that is not just that of faith, or sight in the vision of the blessed. His is a knowledge which can be compared only with that which God the Father has of him. The gospel of John contains many such passages, but this one which points to the sublime reality of Jesus' life with his Father is outstanding in the synoptics. The relationship is unique. Never does Jesus speak of "our Father" referring to us and himself. Speaking of himself, it is always "my Father." In the passage from Chapter 11 just cited, Matthew tells us why.

First Climax: Petrine Text

The next incident (16,13ff) that we note is the expanded confession of faith that Matthew puts in Peter's mouth at Caesarea Philippi. (Cf. Mk 8,27ff; Lk 9,18ff.) Here Jesus' question is a bit different from the formulation in Mark, as is Peter's response and his own reply. "Who do men say that the *Son of Man* is?" gives messianic overtones absent from the other accounts. Peter's inspired response: "You are the Christ, the Son of the living God," seems far more than a mere declaration of messianic status, especially in view of Christ's reaction. "Blessed are you, Simon Bar-Jona, for flesh and blood has not revealed this to you, but my Father in heaven." (16,17) Matthew surely is telling us that Peter was given heavenly help to make his declaration; no such help is narrated in the other accounts which have him proclaim simply the Messiaship of Jesus. This "Son of Man" is Daniel's heavenly being, but he is more than any Jew had ever dreamed he would be; he is "Son of the living God." Peter, first to be gifted with this insight into the mystery of Jesus, is designated the rock on which the new Temple of living stones is to be built. Protestant Christians, following Luther, have been so impressed with this act of divine faith by Simon Peter that they have interpreted the entire passage as a reference to his faith and not his person—so strong in meaning is this passage found in Matthew alone.

Vision of the Judgment

Another significant section of this gospel is the description of the last judgment in Chapter 25. The Son of Man will come in his majesty, sit on the throne of his glory, and separate the sheep from the goats.

> Then the king will say to those on his right hand, "Come, blessed of my Father, take possession of the kingdom prepared for you from the foundation of the world; for I was hungry and you gave me to eat; I was thirsty and you gave me to drink. . . ." Then the just will answer him, saying, "Lord, when did we see you hungry and feed you . . . ?" And answering, the king will say to them, "Amen I say to you, as long as you did it for one of these, the least of my brethren, you did it for me." (25,34ff)

The Son of Man will be "the king" judging all nations—a prerogative of God alone. On a man's attitude toward this king will depend his eternal fate: either everlasting enjoyment of the eternal kingdom of the Father or everlasting punishment in fire. Who, then, can this judge be?

Lest his Christian readers be so caught up in this vision as to forget the human reality, Matthew's narrative immediately brings us back to Jesus' prediction, "The Son of Man will be delivered up to be crucified." (26,2) This sufferer is the same as the Son of Man of the vision—so mighty and yet so mortal. In Gethsemani he undergoes his agony unto death; here the finiteness of his humanity is so clear, in this struggle in his all too human will, that we might be led to doubt his divinity.

> He began to be saddened and exceedingly troubled . . . And going forward a little, he fell prostrate and prayed, saying, "Father, if it is possible, let this cup pass away from me; yet not as I will, but as you will. . . . My Father, if this cup cannot pass away unless I drink it, your will be done" . . . He went back again, and prayed a third time, saying the same words over. (26,37ff)

He is like to us in his prayer, persevering in asking despite difficulties and seeming silence. His human will accepts his Father's will, even though the cup of sorrow which is his passion overflows with fear and pain and the bitterness of unrequited love. His human feelings shrink from such suffering; his human will instinctively would refuse, were he not completely in control of himself. He seems to pray after this fashion: "Not my will, my all too human will. But again, my will, my strong human will, completely dedicated to your divine will. You wish me to fear the pain now, as I shall feel it later. Your will be done in me, my Father, for this is my will, too."

Second Climax

Before the high priest, Jesus makes the same claim in Matthew that he made in Mark and Luke: he is the Messia, yet more than that. "I say to you, hereafter you shall see the Son of Man sitting at the right hand of the Power and coming upon the clouds of heaven." (26,64) The passers-by at Calvary jeered at him, saying, "You who destroy the Temple, and in three days build it up again, save yourself! If you are the Son of God, come down from the cross!" The chief priests mocked him and showed that they had well understood his claim before them. "He saved others, himself he cannot save. . . . He trusted in God; let him deliver him now, if he wants him; for he said, 'I am the Son of God.'" (27,40.42f) They put in his mouth a claim that the Scriptures never explicitly record in so many words, but which the entire record clearly proclaims: he is the Son of God uniquely. His last words in Matthew's gospel are also the baptismal formula which is the heritage of the Church, giving the common Name to three: Father, Son, and Holy Spirit. Vincent Taylor writes: "A step has been taken which was to find its culmination in the Christology of Nicaea." (*The Person of Christ in New Testament Teaching* [London: Macmillan, 1958], p. 16)

LUKE'S OTHER BOOK

This gospel of the synoptics is the good news of Jesus in the form of Christian teaching, *didachē*. In preaching form, *kērygma*, it is found in interesting sections of Luke's second book, The Acts of the Apostles, where we catch sight and almost sound of the original joyful proclamation by the apostles of Jesus of Nazareth as Lord and Savior of all men. This *kērygma* is given to various audiences and varies accordingly, being suited to the background and expectations of the hearers. For Cornelius, the God-fearing Roman centurion, Peter preaches thus:

> Now I really understand that God is not a respecter of persons, but in every nation he who fears him and does what is right is acceptable to him. He sent his word to the children of Israel, preaching peace through Jesus Christ (who is Lord of all). You know what took place throughout Judea; for he began in Galilee after the baptism preached by John: how God anointed Jesus of Nazareth with the Holy Spirit and with power, and he went about doing good and healing all who were in the power of the devil; for God was with him . . . and yet they killed him, hanging him on a tree. But God raised him up on the third day and caused him to be plainly seen, not by all the people, but by witnesses designated beforehand by God, that is, by us, who ate and drank with him after he had risen from the dead. And he charged us to preach to the people and to testify that he it is who has been appointed by God to be judge of the living and of the dead. To him all the prophets bear witness, that through his name all who believe in him may receive forgiveness of sins. (Ac 10,34–43)

Many themes are present here, and all should be noted. Christ is "Lord of all" and appointed judge of the living and the dead. This is the same Jesus as he of Mark's account, baptized, gifted with the power of God, working in Galilee and then in Jerusalem where he was killed. His resurrection, however, is the great fact the apostles are to give witness to, as the prophets had borne witness to him earlier. His name now is the saving sign to all believers. This, then, is the post-Pentecostal faith of the apostles: *Jesus is Lord of all.* The name "Jesus" stands for him who is now identified as *Kýrios, Dominus.* Commitment to belief in this name is now the means of salvation from sin. Baptism in his name (10,48) is an early Christian form, along with the Matthaean trinitarian formula. Peter does not call him "God" directly and explicitly, since in the New Testament the word *theós* is confined either almost exclusively, or exclusively, to the Father. He believes, however, in his divinity. This is the faith of the new Israel, Christ's Church.

Peter's Sermon

The account of Ac 10,34–43, totally Markan in spirit, is followed by what has been called "the gentile Pentecost." (10,44) The Jews' Pentecost related in 2,2–4 is followed by Peter's first sermon, to "men of Israel" from Judea and "every nation on earth"—the Jews of the diaspora. To them, he cites the prophet Joel:

> And it shall come to pass in the last days . . . that I will pour forth of my Spirit upon all flesh. . . . And I will show wonders . . . and signs. . . . Before the day of the Lord comes. . . . And it shall come to pass that whoever calls upon the name of the Lord shall be saved. (Jl 3,1–5)

Peter's account of Jesus' life stresses their Jewish ideas and experience.

> Jesus of Nazareth was a man approved by God among you by miracles and wonders and signs, which God did through him in the midst of you, as you yourselves know. Him, when delivered up by the settled purpose and foreknowledge of God, you have crucified and slain by the hands of wicked men. But God has raised him up. . . . This Jesus God has raised up, and we are all witnesses of it. Therefore, exalted by the right hand of God, and receiving from the Father the promise of the Holy Spirit, he has poured forth this Spirit which you see and hear. . . . Therefore, let all the house of Israel know most assuredly that God has made both Lord and Christ, this Jesus whom you crucified. (Ac 2,22–24.32f.36)

This must be one of the most fundamental testimonies to the way in which the apostles preached the gospel to their fellow Jews. The humanity of Jesus is evident, for they themselves had known him and had delivered him up to be crucified. "This man" who had seemed only such to them during his mortal life has now been raised up by God, first from the empty tomb and then to the very throne of God, whence he sends his promised Spirit to work the wonders of the Last Days. David had given witness to this, and now the apostles do so. Again, there is the primitive Christian formula of divine 51 faith: this Jesus is both Lord, *Kýrios*, and Christ, *Messia*. God has revealed him to be such by exalting him. The *kērygma* pierces through to the hearts of three thousand, who accept baptism in Jesus' name. The Christian community is formed, and is nourished by the teaching, *didachē,* of the apostles and the "breaking of bread." (2,42) The latter is probably the commemoration of the last supper. Jesus is the source and center of both teaching and meal, as he is of their prayers.

The Preaching

In preaching Jesus in these early days, the disciples used the Suffering Servant theme of Isaia 52,13—53,12, as Jesus himself had used it, to try to make them see that he was to suffer and die in Jerusalem for his people. Their Spirit-born faith now enables them to see clearly the plan whereby the God of Abraham and Isaac and Jacob "has glorified his Son Jesus . . . the author of life." (3,13.15) His death is attributed to the ignorance of the Jews and their leaders, but it is God's way of fulfilling the prophecies about the suffering Christ. The theme from Isaia is repeated in 4,27 and notably in 8,26—40, where the deacon Philip "beginning from this scripture, preached Jesus" to the Ethiopian so effectively that baptism was requested and administered. The passage is also noteworthy for containing a very early example of express Christian faith (8,37), though the verse is missing from some of the better manuscripts,

> The eunuch said, "See, here is water; what is there to prevent my being baptized?" And Philip said, "If you believe with all your heart, you may." And he answered and said, "I believe Jesus Christ to be the Son of God." (8,36—38)

No doubt this is that baptism in Jesus' name of which Peter spoke—acceptance of him as God's own Son, in whose name alone a man can be saved.

Stephen

Another deacon, Stephen, who was a Jew from outside Palestine and therefore called a Hellenist, used other Old Testament themes in preaching Jesus to the Jews. Luke draws many parallels between him and the Savior, for Stephen is the first martyr-hero of the Church modeled on the fearless Son of Man. Stephen is the only one in Acts who calls Christ by this messianic title used so often by Jesus in conjunction with his passion and resurrection. Stephen occasions his own suffering and death by telling his enemies of seeing "the glory of God, and Jesus standing at the right hand of God; and he said, 'Behold, I see the heavens opened, and the Son of Man standing at the right hand of God.'" (7,55f) Outside the city, like his Master, they put him to death, with "a young man named Saul" watching their coats. Later this same young man will carry the gospel of Jesus as Stephen preached it, the gospel of salvation for all men whether Jew or Greek, to the ends of the earth. For now, he observes the stoning and hears the final words of a man dying for one for whom Saul was later to die: "Lord Jesus, receive my spirit . . . Lord, do not lay this sin against them." (7,59f) How closely Stephen, the firstfruits of the Church's sacrificial love, parallels him who was the first-fruits of God's creative love. Forgiveness of enemies and prayer for them marks him even as they kill him. Luke had made a similar report of the dying Christ. (Lk 23,34)

Luke's story of Stephen's trial is closely modeled on Jesus' own. (6,12–7,60) False witnesses accused him, though their charge could have been true. Stephen did preach and teach that Jesus of Nazareth was the fulfillment of the Mosaic Law, as also of the Temple and its cult; these were themes of the synoptics, as we have seen. To the Jews he speaks of their great forefathers and prophets, of Abraham and Joseph, of Moses above all, whom "God sent to be ruler and redeemer," and who said to them, "God will raise up to you a prophet from among your brethren." (Dt 18,15) Stephen also spoke of Joshua, of David, of Solomon who built the Temple. He reminds the onlookers that the covenant with Abraham was the first and continuing sign of God's love, so that the Mosaic Law and the Temple itself were only further expressions of it—expressions that have now come to term and full meaning in Jesus, "the Just One" whom Israel has betrayed and murdered. His is the first attempt at a Christian theology of the Old Testament and of history. It ends with his act of faith in the *Lord* Jesus, the same Lord as the God of Israel, faithful to his promises throughout time.

Not by mere accident does Luke connect the martyrdom of this most Christlike figure with the persecution of the Church in Jerusalem and the consequent scattering of Christians over Judea and Samaria. The teaching of Stephen, enacted heroically, is that Christ belongs to all nations and not merely to the Jews of Jerusalem.

Saul–Paul

And now Luke brings back that youth who had watched and heard, that Saul who probably had never conversed with Jesus but hated his name, hated those who belonged to his Church, and persecuted them with all his zeal. (8,3) His conversion will be the turning-point in the history of the early Church. It is told in terms of his act of faith on the road to Damascus. Lying there in the road, he sees a light and hears a voice, " 'Saul, Saul, why do you persecute me?' And he said, 'Who are you, Lord?' And he said, 'I am Jesus . . . whom you are persecuting.' . . . And he, trembling and amazed, said, 'Lord, what will you have me do?' " (9,4–6) Sight of the risen Jesus has given him the faith of the apostles: Jesus is *Lord*. He will devote his life to preaching this truth that has not been revealed to him by flesh and blood.

CHAPTER SIX

CHRIST IN ST. PAUL
AND ST. JOHN

PAUL'S PERSONAL WITNESS

In "Acts"

The former Saul of Tarsus, pupil of Gamaliel in Jerusalem and zealous persecutor of Christians, became Paul, apostle to the gentiles and first theologian of the Church. Acts relates the Damascus vision three times (9,3–19; 22,6–21; 26,12–18), in which the risen Christ, now manifested as Lord by the glorious light that shone from him, gave Saul the gift of faith. This faith was to be perfected by his baptism in the name of the same Lord. From this point on, Saul uses the now familiar formula of faith when he urges Jews and gentiles to turn to God in repentance and "believe in our Lord Jesus Christ." (20,21) It is a divine revelation that he preaches, as his witness in Gal 1,15–16 makes clear: ". . . when it pleases him who from my mother's womb set me apart and called me by his grace, to reveal his Son in me, that I might preach him among the gentiles." Paul believes that the Jesus he proclaims is the Son of God; in the speeches related in Luke's book of Acts he preaches Jesus as the Lord. "Lord" means "God" for him.

To the Jews

At Antioch in Pisidia, speaking to Jews in the synagogue (Ac 13,16–41), Paul dwells on the same themes as Stephen and Peter in their speeches. Jesus, of David's royal line, is the Savior sent to the Jews first but rejected by them, although accepted by God who raised him up from the dead. Paul who knew only the risen Christ saw the day of his resurrection as the decisive revelation of his divinity. To this day of glory he applies the phrase of Ps 2,7: "You are my son, this day I have begotten you." Forgiveness of sin is proclaimed to all who believe in this risen Christ, God's son.

To the Gentiles

In Athens, speaking to Epicureans, Stoics, and bystanders generally at the Areopagus, Paul identifies their Unknown God with the God of Israel and Christianity, Creator and Lord of all things. This common God of all is calling all men to repentance, for men are to be judged with justice "by a Man whom he has appointed, and whom he has guaranteed to all by raising him from the dead." (17,31) Again, this is the Christ whom Paul preached: the risen Christ, a "man" all the same, completely human, but sharing qualities which belong to God alone.

For preaching the resurrection of Jesus and of all men, Paul was almost killed by Asian Jews. He was put on trial before the Sanhedrin when he reiterated the central fact of his preaching: "It is about the hope and the resurrection of the dead that I am on trial." (23,6) This for Paul is all the difference between life and death, between darkness and light; his own destiny is to be a suffering servant of God in imitation of Christ. (26,16; cf. Col 1,24.)

I stand here to testify to both high and low, saying nothing beyond what the prophets and Moses said would come to pass: that the Christ was to suffer, that he first by his resurrection from the dead was to proclaim light to the people and to the gentiles. (26,22f)

Paul proclaimed that light and did it in Rome where he had insisted they take him, for he was born a citizen of the Empire. Luke gives a homey picture of him in the center of that world, trying all day long to convince the leading Jews that Jesus is the fulfillment of the Law and the prophets. We can surely draw some consolation, as well as instruction, from the fact that "some believed what was said, and some disbelieved." (28,24) Even Paul had to wait for the grace of faith to strike his audience. He could not construct an absolutely compelling argument from the Old Testament (cf. Chapter 3), any more than we. Luke leaves him there in his house in Rome, welcoming all who come to him, "preaching the kingdom of God and teaching about the Lord Jesus Christ with all boldness and unhindered." (28,31) This is Luke's last word to us; it repeats the early Christian theme that the kingdom of God is here. Jesus Christ is Lord!

Paul's Witness in His Writings

The Lordship of Jesus is the dominating idea in Paul's theology. For him it expresses perfectly the religious attitude of Christians toward him whose name they bear, once they have been baptized in that name. He calls Christ "Son" (of God) about seventeen times in his letters; twice perhaps he uses the word "God" of him. He terms Jesus "Lord" about two hundred and twenty-two times. Remember, he was not primarily proving a proposition or arguing a point in these letters; he was pouring out his Christian faith in his own way, to help other Christians deepen their faith and to understand better the mystery of the risen Jesus and his way. It is the way of service to God and others for love of God, despite the sufferings entailed. Joy in the sufferings is included, for suffering makes a man more like the Lord Jesus who through obedient suffering won his glorious name.

Philippians 2,6–11

This theme is constant in Paul's writings, but it is never more eloquent or affecting than in the rhythmic passage in Phil 2,6–11 which gives us a glimpse into the early Christians' worship service. Almost certainly this section of Paul's letter is his version of a Christian hymn in use around the years 40–45 A.D. in Syrian Antioch or Palestine. We know from the Roman Pliny that first-century Christians gathered "to sing a song (*carmen*) to Christ as to a god." (*Epistulae*, 10.96) If this is one such hymn, we are in liturgical contact here with the first Christians, our brothers like us in many ways but none more so than in this common faith.

Paul has been speaking in ordinary terms of the daily Christian life. He returns to his moralizing theme after verse 11. But in between lies this inspiring purple patch of deepest insight and faith.

[Christ] Who, while he kept his character as God,
did not consider his divine equality
something to be proudly paraded.

No, he despoiled himself,
by taking on the Servant's character,
becoming similar to mortal men.

And looking outwardly like any other man,
he carried self-abasement, through obedience,
right up to death, yes, death by the Cross.

Therefore did God in turn immeasurably exalt him,
and graciously bestow on him the Name,
outweighing every other name;

that everyone, at Jesus' Name,
should bow adoring, those in heaven,
on earth, in the infernal regions,

and every tongue take up the cry,
"Jesus is Lord,"
thus glorifying God his Father.

(Phil 2,6–11; tr. by David M. Stanley, S.J., CBQ 20 [1958], 180)

We can almost hear the triumphant chant at the end: "Jesus is Lord." This is the simplest form of the early creed, the expression of the Christians' belief in salvation through him whose name is now recognized as a divine Name. To the Romans Paul would later write: "For if you confess in speech that Jesus is the Lord, and believe in your heart that God has raised him from the dead, you shall be saved." (10,9) The hymn from Philippians is one example of how the community there renewed their oral profession of faith at their services. We treasure it for that, as well as for its dogmatic implications, which are many. A number of these follow.

KÉNŌSIS   Paul here clearly speaks of a Christ who pre-existed his earthly sojourn, for "he *kept* his character as God." Obviously, therefore, he had possessed it before. In our study of the New Testament up until now, we have not found this pre-existent Christ mentioned. Paul and John are especially gifted with this insight into divine revelation. This Christ, who had always had the nature of God and who retained it undiminished during his earthly life, gave up the external manifestation of his divinity by "despoiling himself" of it. This *kénōsis* (the Greek term for "despoiling") consisted first in the incarnation itself—when this one who is God took on the human character of the Servant prophesied in Is 52,13–53,12. In early Christian days, the incarnation was thought of more as a humiliation of God than as an

57

exaltation of man. He became like us. He looked like us. Perhaps Paul had the glorified and glorious face of the risen Christ in mind, the transfigured Christ of the Damascus road, as the contrast to his appearance in the days of his flesh. The wonder then for Paul is: he looked like *any* man.

The second *kénōsis,* or the second stage of it, was the historic life of Christ, again to Paul's mind and that of the early hymnodists, a surprisingly lowly life in spite of the miracles and wonders wrought by the Master. They dwelt, as we must, on his filial obedience all through his life, until the cross crowned such love with death. Thus far the hymn concerns the downward movement of God to man, the "descending" so familiar to John, as we shall see. Now the hymn reverses the movement; this same obedience has merited for him an exaltation without limit—resurrection from the dead, ascension to the right hand of God in a majesty that was his before the self-despoiling.

In glory his name is "Jesus," the name he bore on earth as son of Mary. This Jesus receives for his loving obedience the holy name *Kýrios* which manifests him for what he has always been—universal Lord, divine in power, adorable and to be adored by all. As once God changed Jacob's name to Israel (Gn 32,29), connoting in popular etymology a "striving with God," and Jesus himself changed Simon's name to Kepha, "Rock" (Mt 16,18), so now Jesus of Nazareth, the carpenter son of Mary (and Joseph, as men supposed) receives that name which up to now has belonged to Yahweh alone: *Lord.* For those who sing the Christian hymn the reason can only be that Jesus *is* Lord, equal to Yahweh.

"KÝRIOS"   In the early Christians' Septuagint translation of the Old Testament into Greek, the title *Kýrios* translates Yahweh or some form of Elohim 6432 times, as against the two hundred fifteen times it is used of someone other than God.* The Psalms, the prayers of these devout Jews, are filled with the phrase, *"Lord* God" of Israel. They use the titles "Lord" and "God" interchangeably, as anyone browsing through the Psalter will immediately perceive. To take this title from the Temple hymns and attribute it to Jesus, as they did, marks a complete revolution in their religious faith, brought about by God's saving grace. "Jesus is Lord" is their joyous cry, their prayer of appreciation to the Father who sent him. Their hymn ends, as it began, with God.

Reread Phil 2,6–11 slowly and try to take in its flavor. You might even pray it a few times. "All whatsoever you do, in word or in work, do in the name of the Lord Jesus Christ, giving thanks to God and the Father by Jesus Christ our Lord." (Col 3,17)

One last word about this hymn. There is a school of "kenotic" theologians deriving from nineteenth-century Russia which interprets the "despoiling" as a loss of godhead for the time of Christ's earthly life. According

---

* Cf. Hatch-Redpath, *A Concordance to the Septuagint* (New York: Oxford University Press, 1897), Vol. II, pp. 800-839.

to them, the Son of God gave up "being God" for those thirty-odd years, and was only man. His merely human virtue, especially his sacrificial love of God and of others even to the cross, merited for him the resumption of his godhead after the resurrection-ascension. These theologians were (and are) godly men who mistakenly try to accommodate the incarnation to the evolutionary science of the time, especially to the newly popular social psychology. Their starting-point of course is scriptural. *"Kénōsis"* legitimately has for them the meaning indicated above unless the living Church should say otherwise, as in fact the Church does. The Russian mystical stream of the saint as "poor man," of whom Christ is the supreme type, has been strongly contributory here.

The Jesus of the New Testament, however, simply does not fit such a *"kénōsis,"* the Church repeatedly says. Both existentially and psychologically (that is, with respect to his human psyche), Christ remained God while he became man. The Son of Mary testified that he was the Son of God. He did not leave his divinity behind when he came to earth for us and for our salvation. From the Pauline hymn of Philippians 2 the kenotic theologians get only their name, not their theory; verse 6 condemns them with the Greek word *hypárchōn*—"being in the state of God." The descent is made by one who is God. The incarnation is the incarnation of a divine person.

Christ's True Humanity

We have considered this hymn at length because it is unique in the New Testament revelation about our Savior. In Paul, as in John, Christ's divinity is so completely taken for granted and so frequently required by the sense of what is written that an extended study of the pertinent texts would demand a shelf of books. As we have seen, ordinarily Paul uses the title "Lord" for Jesus as divine, and "Christ" as a proper name. He does not stress the earthly life of our Lord much, although he testifies to it. His Christ is no mythical figure like Mithra or Adonis. The only time Paul mentions our Lady is in Gal 4,4: "But when the fullness of time came, God sent his Son, born of a woman, born under the Law, that he might redeem those who were under the Law. . . ." The next event in Christ's life of which he makes mention is the last supper. (1 Cor 11,23ff) The present liturgical service is modeled primarily on his account of this central event of salvation. He speaks of course, of Christ's death, resurrection, and ascension, but of those first thirty-some years he has almost nothing to say.

All the same, Paul has no doubt whatever of the true humanity of Jesus whom he calls the "second Adam." (Rom 5,14–21; 1 Cor 15,21ff) The first man, created as an image of God and in his likeness, brought sin and death to the world through his disobedience; the Second Adam, inserted into that same race by a virgin's "Be it done . . ." as the "image of the invisible God" (Col 1,15), brought superabundant grace and life to men through his obedience. The tree of the knowledge of good and evil brought forth fruit for mankind's fall; the tree of the cross bore the firstfruits of all creation's rising: him

59

in whom "dwells all the fullness of the Godhead, bodily." (Col 2,9)

Paul the theologian furnishes us with these insights into the mystery of Jesus, God and man simultaneously. "There is one God, and one Mediator between God and men, himself man, Christ Jesus. . . ." (1 Tim 2,5) In stressing the humanity of Jesus Paul does not forget his divinity, but he usually states it in terms other than "God." That name is almost always reserved for the Father. But on a few occasions Paul seems to have used the word *theós* for Jesus, either in constructions where without the article it should be translated "divine" or where God manifests himself in Christ.

Titus 2,13

One of these places is Ti 2,13. There God's loving kindness is spoken of as appearing to all men, instructing us to live justly, "looking for the blessed hope and glorious coming of our great God and Savior Jesus Christ, who gave himself for us. . . ." Some deny that the text really identifies this "great God" with Jesus, their chief reason being that Paul does not do so in other places. They seem to leave no room for any unusual mode of speaking by the apostle. The great modern form-critic Rudolf Bultmann, interestingly, allows this as one of the two places where Paul speaks of Christ as "God." The Clementine Vulgate (1592) inserts a comma after "Savior," but A. Merk (1938) after "God," which would require in translation, "and of our Savior. . . ."

Romans 9,5

Another place is Rom 9,5: ". . . [the Israelites] who have the fathers, and from whom is the Christ according to the flesh, who is, over all things, God blessed forever. Amen." The last phrase of this doxology may be addressed to God the Father, obviously, since codices of the New Testament are without punctuation and do not furnish evidence either way, beyond what is usual in Greek construction. Some Catholic scholars like Cerfaux and Huby do not think that the passage refers to Christ; perhaps we had best simply instance it and go on.

Paul wrote such wonderful things of the Word incarnate that a textual doubt surely cannot make us doubt his complete faith in Christ as Son of God, *the* Son. In that same letter to the Romans, he writes:

> By sending his Son in the likeness of sinful flesh as a sin-offering, he [God] has condemned sin in the flesh. . . . [8,3] For those whom he has foreknown he has also predestined to become conformed to the image of his Son, that he should be the firstborn among many brethren. . . . He who has not spared even his own Son, but has delivered him for us all. . . . Who shall separate us from the love of Christ? Shall tribulation, or distress, or persecution, or hunger, or nakedness,

or danger, or the sword? . . . For I am sure that neither death, nor life, nor angels, nor principalities, nor things present, nor things to come, nor powers, nor height, nor depth, nor any other creature will be able to separate us from the love of God, which is in Christ Jesus our Lord. (8,29.32.35.37–39)

Such words need no comment, surely; they challenge us to believe in Christ as Paul did, and to prove our belief by our lives.

To the Hebrews

In taking leave of the great apostle of the gentiles, we could hardly do better than look at the magnificent opening of the letter "To the Hebrews," which is surely Pauline in spirit if not (as is equally sure) written by Paul himself. In reading this, we hear accents a bit different from those we have heard from Paul, but we know the ideas are from him.

God, who at sundry times and in divers manners spoke in times past to the fathers by the prophets, last of all in these days has spoken to us by his Son, whom he appointed heir of all things, by whom also he made the world; who, being the brightness of his glory and the image of his substance, and upholding all things by the word of his power, has effected man's purgation from sin and, taken his seat at the right hand of the Majesty on high, having become so much superior to the angels as he has inherited a more excellent name than they. (1,1–4)

The Pauline themes are there, but also the sublime expressions closely connected with the inspired writings of St. John, to whom we now go for the final "words of eternal life" of the New Testament.

JOHN'S WITNESS

These words of John are written "that you may [continue to] believe that Jesus is the Christ, the Son of God, and that believing you may have life in his name." (20,31; the original ending of this gospel. Chapter 21 is a later addition, Johannine and inspired.) John's purpose, then, is the same as that of the synoptic writers: to deepen the faith of his Christian readers. Like them, too, he selects his material out of the multiple words and works of Jesus that as an eyewitness he had seen and now remembers under the illumining inspiration of the Spirit. Jesus had promised this Consoler, who now dwells in the Church—the Spirit of Truth who would teach all the truth. (16,13) Not by accident does John end his gospel with the profession of faith of Thomas the apostle: "My Lord and my God!" (20,28) This is the personal commitment toward which he is leading all his readers: to acknowledge Jesus of Nazareth as both Christ (Messia) and Son of God (Lord, in the sense of God). Only thus will a man have life, true life for eternity. Blessed are those who believe, Christ says—his final pronouncement of beatitude upon us who have not yet seen him face to face.

Its Differences

Any careful reading of this gospel, however brief, will serve to show how different it is from the other three in tone and content. The divinity of Jesus, far from being only obscurely and gradually revealed, is stated and restated. Few miracles are mentioned, entire new discourses are given, metaphors seem to take the place of titles for Jesus: lamb of God, bread of life, way-truth-life, resurrection and life, door, good shepherd, vine, light of the world. Only vague hints of such ideas had been given in the synoptics. Is this the same "gospel" concerning the same Jesus? In essence, yes.

Its Similarities

John is writing of the same man from Nazareth and of his historical life. He begins with the baptism by John, describes the ministry of Jesus—mainly in Jerusalem, with only Chapters 2 and 6 clearly set in Galilee—speaks of journeys, especially to Jerusalem for the annual feasts of the Jews, and concludes with the passion-resurrection narrative as do the other gospel writers. But in stressing the circumstances of Jesus' life and that of the Church, the fourth evangelist dwells on things not stressed in the earlier gospels. Above all he underscores the ending of the former covenant centered in the Temple of Jerusalem, and its replacement by the new covenant centered in the body of Christ. John's drama has Jerusalem, represented by the Temple authorities, reject Jesus, thereby losing her ability to save men. Jesus in turn by his life, death, and resurrection replaces the Temple as God's favored dwelling place on earth, and becomes the source of salvation for all men. For Christians now, the covenant of the new Jerusalem is in Jesus' glorified body, for he is the Lord. This accounts for Thomas's cry of faith, "My Lord and my God." (Jn 20,28)

Divisions

The fourth gospel is conveniently divided by Dodd, Brown, and others into a Prologue (1,1–18), a Book of Signs (1,19–12,50), and a Book of Glory or of the Passion-Resurrection (13,1–21,25). Since the prologue is John's final reflection on the rest of what he wrote, we shall leave it to the end of our consideration and begin with the Book of Signs.

THE BOOK OF SIGNS   This opens with the questioning of the Baptist by the Jews and his denial that he is the Messia. The theme is set. The Messia is to be revealed in Jesus, the lamb of God pointed out by John to his disciples. But this lamb will be rejected and slain as a paschal sacrifice by the authorities of the Temple. Jesus is recognized as Rabbi or Master (1,38), the Messia or Christ (1,39), the one prophesied by Moses (1,45), the Son of God and King of Israel (1,49). So quickly does John summarize the long process of dawning faith that we have seen in the synoptics! This highly compressed catalogue of titles accorded to Jesus by perfect Pentecostal faith is climaxed by his own view of himself. He implies that he is greater than the patriarch Jacob (Israel) from whom the people takes its name. The commerce with heaven of the former covenant is as nothing compared with what they will see if they remain faithful to Jesus.

In John's gospel only one "sign," that of the water-wine of Cana, is enough to manifest his glory and win the belief of the disciples.

THE BOOK OF GLORY   The "glory" of Jesus is John's way of describing his divinity; perhaps we would say for glory his "majesty." In the Old Testament the *kebhod Yahweh* was the special manifestation of God on earth—the light that shone in the pillar of fire on the desert. Later it was understood as the *shekinah,* the wondrous light that manifested God's presence in the Holy of Holies of the Temple. Its reflection shone from Moses' face, therefore the Israelites could not keep looking at him. (Ex 34,29–35; 2 Cor 3,7–16) St. John uses the same word glory with respect to Jesus. His glory is manifested in his miracles, in his passion which is a lifting up from the earth to manifest the truth of God to men, in his resurrection. "We have seen his glory," he affirms (1,14), and it has cast its light upon the evangelist's entire life. For him the incarnation is not a "despoiling" of Jesus' godly attributes but is rather the translucent revelation of the godhead through the assumed humanity of Jesus. "He who sees me sees also the Father." (14,9) The majesty and glory of God shine from the face of Jesus, as Paul had seen. (2 Cor 4,4.6) Now every act, every word of his manifests the truth that God is love.

JESUS' HUMANITY   The great glory of God made manifest in Jesus does not by any means blind St. John to his humanity. The central theological affirmation of this gospel is, "The Word was made flesh" (1,14), that is, human. The Docetists, heretics of John's time, were already asserting that the incarnation simply could not have taken place, that God may have appeared (*dokein*) in Jesus of Nazareth but that the humanity of Jesus was just a phantasm. To silence any such denials of the Lord's full human status, John said in his first epistle,

> I write of what was from the beginning, what we have heard, what we have seen with our eyes, what we have looked upon and our hands have handled: of the Word of Life . . . , the Life Eternal, which was with the Father and has appeared to us. (1 Jn 1,1.2)

True, his gospel is a spiritual interpretation of the life of Jesus and filled with the transcendent qualities ascribed to Jesus: equality with the Father (5,17–

18), eternity (8,58), unique knowledge of the Father (10,15; 17,25), sinlessness (8,46), absolute unity with the Father. (10,30.38; 14,9; 17,21) But John never lets this divine aspect of Christ absorb or overpower the human.

In Life.   Jesus grows weary (4,6), feels thirst (4,7), weeps at the tomb of Lazarus (11,35), washes his disciples' feet (13,5), serves them bread and fish. (21,13) Above all, he undergoes his passion (the New Testament term for sufferings and death), and the triumph of his resurrection in a truly human body and soul. Early in this gospel he has said: "Destroy this temple, and in three days I shall raise it up." (2,19) The Jews said they could not grasp his meaning, but the disciples knew after the event what he had intended. "He was speaking of the temple of his body. When, accordingly, he had risen from the dead, his disciples remembered. . . ." (2,21f)

In Death.   The presence of God in the Temple at Jerusalem was to yield to his presence in Jesus Christ, the new Temple of the new covenant. On the cross, his body was opened by the point of the soldier's lance; blood and water, symbols of baptism and the eucharist, flowed forth for the life of the Church and the world. The paschal lamb was slain to take away the sins of the world. (1, 29; cf. Ex 12,46.) There is no doubt about a body so pierced, or a heart so wounded in death. John felt so strongly on this that he could write,

> This is he who came in water and in blood, Jesus Christ. . . . Everyone who believes that Jesus is the Christ is born of God. . . . Whoever confesses that Jesus is the Son of God, God abides in him and he in God. . . . Every spirit that confesses that Jesus Christ has come in the flesh, is of God. (1 Jn 5,6; 5,1; 4,15; 4,2)

For John, there is no difference between the Jesus of history and the Christ of his faith; they are the same. At the washing of feet he has Christ say: "You call me Master and Lord and you say well, for so I am." (13,13) The Lord gives an example of true dominion. He serves others out of love.

Jesus as Mediator.   This Christ is the link between heaven and earth, joining in his person "all that the Father has" and all that we are. Israel's eponymous tribal ancestor, Jacob, had seen a ladder stretching from earth to heaven with angels ascending and descending on it. Jesus uses the picture in describing himself. "You shall see heaven opened, and the angels of God ascending and descending upon the Son of Man." (1,51) Only God can bridge the gap between the Infinite and finite man. He has done so in sending his Son. "No one has ascended into heaven except him who has descended from heaven: the Son of Man who is in heaven." (3,13) He became man that man might become God (the usual phrase of the Fathers to describe new life). He is the way, the only way to the Father. (14,6) At the supper he reminds the disciples, "I came forth from the Father and have come into the world. Again I leave the world and go to the Father." (16,28) It is important for us that he go, for thereby he will show us how all men are to be saved—by rising to newness of life in God. He is the resurrection and the life. His life is always with the Father, but it includes the descent of his incarnation, the raising up on the cross, the descent into the tomb, the rising of the resurrection-ascension, and the final sending of his Spirit. That Spirit of truth will glorify him, because he will receive of what is his, and will declare it to the disciples. (16,14)

For this Jesus prayed at the supper.

> Father . . . glorify your Son, that your Son may glorify you, even as you have given him power over all flesh, in order that to all those you have given him he may give everlasting life. Now this is eternal life, that they may know you, the only true God, and Jesus Christ, whom you have sent. (17,1–3)

The life that he gives is the life of the Spirit, a life of truth. It marks Jesus out as God, who alone is master of human life and death. (Cf. Is 45,7f.) "As the Father has life in himself, even so he has given to the Son also to have life in himself. . . ." (5,26) This divine power Jesus dramatized in the raising of his friend Lazarus, a crucial event in his life for it led to belief for many but also to preparations for his end. (11,53)

Surely the scene in Chapter 6 is anticipatory. "Unless you eat the flesh of the Son of Man, and drink his blood, you shall not have life in you. He who eats my flesh and drinks my blood has life everlasting and I will raise him up on the last day." (6,54f.) His living body is the Temple of the living God; his eucharistic body will be the manna of the new covenant, the life-giving bread of the Spirit. When many left him rather than accept this "hard saying," he drew from Peter the cry: "Lord, to whom shall we go? You have words of everlasting life, and we have come to believe and to know that you are the Christ, the Son of God." (6,69f.)

Jesus' Claim   Uniquely in the gospels, John has the "Jews," the hostile Temple authorities, understanding that he is claiming to be the Son of God in a natural way, and rebelling at the thought. When he defends his miracle-working on the Sabbath, explaining that his Father continues his creative work then and so does he, they are anxious to put him to death: "He not only broke the Sabbath, but also called God his own Father, making himself equal to God." (5,18) When he claimed God for his Father in a way superior to theirs and used a form of the divine name Yahweh in replying to them ("Before Abraham came to be, *I am*"), they took up stones to throw at him. (8,58f) Stoning was their punishment for blasphemy.

Again they took up stones against him at the Feast of Dedication or 65 Hanukkah (10,22–39) for saying, "I and the Father are one" (one *thing*, in

Greek). This describes a unity such as exists between no two others, not even two in one flesh, who remain independent and individual even in their love. "We stone you for blasphemy, and because you, being a man, make yourself God." (10,33) Well did his enemies remember this claim, and use it at his trial. "We have a Law, and according to that Law he must die, because he has made himself Son of God." (19,7) The synoptics never depict his audiences so antagonistic to him, so clearly understanding the significance of his words and works. John has them seeing their dilemma with a perfect clarity: either adore this man as God or crucify him.

We know the horn they took. Darkness resisted light. We know how we, children of light, must answer: he is the true light.

THE PROLOGUE   Looming large among the signs in John's gospel is the theme of the new creation. The prologue is clearly modeled on the opening chapter of Genesis, and many other things about the gospel point to this theme. The seven days are reflected by seven episodes in the Book of Signs, seven miracles related, seven discourses given, seven titles that Jesus gives himself. This is the story of the Creator's second week, resulting in a new world with a new life. Jesus himself is that new creation, the life and light of the new world. His flesh gives life; his teaching gives light. Both are really identified in him, as John saw steadily.

> In the beginning was the Word,
> and the Word was with God;
> and the Word was God.
> All things were made through him,
> and without him was made
> nothing that has been made.
> In him was life,
> and the life was the light of men.
> And the light shines in the darkness;
> and the darkness grasped it not.
>
> It was the true light
> that enlightens every man
> who comes into the world.
> He was in the world
> and the world was made through him,
> and world knew him not.
> He came unto his own,
> and his own received him not.
> But to as many as received him
> he gave the power of becoming sons of God;
> to those who believe in his name:
> Who were born not of blood,
> nor of the will of the flesh,
> nor of the will of man, but of God.

And the Word was made flesh,
and dwelt among us.
And we saw his glory—
glory as of the only-begotten of the Father—
full of grace and truth.

(1,1–5.9–14)

Many Christians are accustomed to read or hear these words and to genuflect at "the Word was made flesh." This is in fact the "last word" in John's gospel, the last word in the entire gospel. It is the highest and deepest penetration into the mystery of the Word incarnate that has been given to mortal men. Here we are in touch with the Word of God, eternally existing with God in the mind of the Father. It is a creative Word whose causality extends to everything. "And the Word was *Theós*." No qualifications here. The Word was God. With this brief sentence John sums up the teaching of Jesus, the effect of Jesus on the religious life of all men. The Word was, and is, and ever will be God.

The Word was made flesh, and dwelt among us. This eternal Word, secure in the heart of the Father, came down and took up his abode with fickle men. He made a new tabernacle of his presence, to replace the desert tent of the Sinai covenant. This new tabernacle is his human flesh for the life and light of the world.

The Word was made flesh—how men had longed for this moment and this revelation without knowing what they were longing for. That the great God would come and save mankind, that he would accomplish this mercy through a man—for this Israel prayed and hoped. But she could not dimly suspect the greatness of his mercy: that he would send his own Son to be born of Jewish flesh, for the light and life of the world. The Word was made flesh.

The tragedy of Israel—God's chosen—lies in this: that her leaders did not recognize him nor welcome him into his world. He came unto his own creation (the Greek pronoun is neuter plural: his own *things*); his own people (the pronouns are masculine, personal) did not accept him. Creatures did; the winds and seas obeyed him and quieted down, diseases disappeared at his word, bread was multiplied, even death was subject to him. But human beings, including his beloved Israel, alone did not acknowledge him as Master and Lord. The poignancy of John's thoughts can only be imagined; he too was of this people, and had begged them to turn from darkness to light.

For John had seen the light, this light of glory that surrounded Jesus in his transfiguration on the mountain, a glory that marked him out as God's only-begotten, "full of grace and truth." So had Yahweh been designated in his Old Testament covenant. (Ex 34,6) Now in the new time, grace and truth come in their fullness through Jesus Christ. He is the new Moses, whose Law is not written on tablets of stone but on the loving hearts of men. The new commandment is this: God is love, and men must be like him in loving. They must be self-sacrificing, generous, understanding. Jesus Christ has revealed this, he who alone could have done so. "Come, Lord Jesus!" (Ap 22,20)

67

CHAPTER SEVEN

CHRIST
IN THE PRE-NICENE
FATHERS

The revelation was now complete. God's Word had been spoken to the world as a person and the world could never be the same again. History's climax had been reached. Man's second chance at salvation was at hand in the Second Adam, Christ, now permanently present in his sacraments and through his Church. The Word remained enfleshed in man's world, spoken and received on the tongues of men.

All Christians were baptized into Christ, into a living faith that Jesus of Nazareth was simultaneously equal to Yahweh and fully human. "Christ is Lord" was their way of expressing this belief. The apostles preached and taught this in season and out of season, enriching the formula with their unique recollections of their years with the Master. Under the influence of the Holy Spirit, the Church community gradually formulated this apostolic preaching and teaching into what we now call the New Testament. This written tradition was accepted as the inspired word of God, of equal value with the pre-Christian Scriptures and able to provide Christians with a human experience of the living God. From those days to this, the Church has spoken in biblical terms to men of all ages, cultures, and climes. The Word of God in his Church, whether committed to writing or otherwise, is universal.

The Problem

But how else to speak of this Word incarnate in the words of fallible men? How to express this burgeoning Christian faith in terms other than a mere repetition of biblical phrases? This was the problem set to the post-apostolic generation of Christian teachers. It is the problem still for preachers and teachers of God's word. We have difficulty in our automotive and automated age in making Israelitic imagery meaningful. Men and women of a nuclear-space-television age do not readily take in symbols from nature and the history of an ancient people. The same difficulty beset the early Christians. We shall see how they tried to solve it.

Their world was of course far different from ours. Roman "peace" would last for another four hundred years, but Greek was still the common language and culture of the Empire: a case of the conquerors themselves conquered. Graeco-Roman polytheism with its anthropomorphic gods would try to make Christ into another humanized god of mythology. Graeco-Roman neo-Platonic philosophy, with its superspiritual notion of God and reality, would never allow for the realism that the incarnation of the Word demands. In this thought system, God was too transcendent to become a Jew, a man with a body like ours. Roman republican religion would find it impossible to find a place for Christ, a god belonging to no civic pantheon and without interest of any sort in imperial affairs. Against such prejudices, Christian teachers had to explain the religion of the God of Israel newly revealed in Christ. This new wine could not be contained in the old bottles of Greek categories or Roman rule. The God-man was something entirely different—and so was the world because of him.

The Jewish world was different, too. Most of the first Christians were converts from Judaism, of course. Their monotheism had to become, by Christian faith, trinitarian monotheism. Some "Judaizers" wanted Jesus to be just another prophet like Moses or Isaia, changing nothing of Old Testament law or rubrics. The apostles preached him, however, not just as a new patch on the old garment of Mosaic Law but as a "new man" to be put on and worn in a completely new life.

HERESIES

Docetism

Even in the apostles' time, strange ideas of Christ were popping up in otherwise Christian communities. One way to contest the truth of the new religion was to claim that Christ had never been truly human. He was a ghostlike figure who seemed to be a human but was in fact a spirit. From the Greek word for "seem," these believers were called Docetists. St. John the evangelist wrote against them in his letters, vindicating the true humanity, body and soul, of Christ. (Cf. 1 Jn 1,1; 4,1; 2 Jn 7.)

Docetists, who are still with us, suspect that the human body is somehow evil because it is corporeal; God who is spirit can have nothing to do with "flesh" except to condemn it. "The Word made flesh" is a scandal to them, so they try to make the body of Christ unreal—as also his sufferings, emotions, birth, and death.

IGNATIUS   Against such attacks the great bishop Ignatius of Antioch protested, on his way to martyrdom at Rome about 107 A.D.:

> But if, as some atheists, that is, unbelievers, say, his suffering was but a make-believe—when in reality they themselves are make-believes— then why am I in chains? Why do I even pray that I may fight with the beast? In vain, then, do I die! My testimony is, after all, but a lie about the Lord. Shun these wildlings, then. . . . (*Epistle to the Trallians*, 10–11)

For him, no ghostlike Christ would do. "Our God Jesus Christ was brought to birth by the Holy Spirit in the womb of Mary, of David's seed, according to God's great plan for men." (*Epistle to the Ephesians*, 18,2)

The creeds were even then being formulated, and echoes of them sound in his phrases: "truly born . . . truly persecuted under Pontius Pilate . . . was truly crucified and died." (*Epistle to the Trallians*, 9) He anticipated the vagaries of later heretics by vindicating the unity of Christ's person, as well as his humanity and divinity. His distinction to express the latter realities was useful at the time and based on St. Paul, but it was to occasion misinterpretation later on. Ignatius used the phrase "according to the flesh" for the humanity, and "according to the spirit" for the divinity of Christ. This terminology was thoroughly in accord with Semitic, that is, biblical, usage. The impression could easily be derived that the manhood of Jesus was corporeal only—all spirituality (in the Greek sense of "spirit") being attributed

70

to godhead. Arius later used just this distinction in his *Logos-sarx* (Word-flesh) Christology.

MARCION   In mid-second century Rome Marcion denied that Christ had a real body, saying that the spirit-Christ was not truly born but appeared suddenly in Tiberius' fifteenth year of rule. A true Docetist, Marcion found suffering incompatible with his idea of God. He therefore denied it to Christ whom he called the Son of the God of the New Testament, clothed only with the outward appearance of a man. Marcion was the son of the bishop of Pontus on the Black Sea and lived to be excommunicated by his father. He came to Rome where he founded his own church. Irenaeus and Tertullian both wrote against him, as we shall see.

Gnosticism

Ordinary Christians went on adoring the God-man in their usual way, repeating the biblical phrases taught them by the apostles and their successor-bishops. A group that had had a considerable history in both pagan and Jewish circles began to appear within the Christian communities, claiming to possess "inside information" about God. They called themselves "Gnostics" from the Greek word for knowledge. It is a New Testament word, of course. Paul speaks frequently of the Christian's *gnōsis* and *sophía*, his knowledge and wisdom of the mystery of God which the revelation made in Christ conveys to him. The Gnostics claimed to be the only complete Christians, gifted with a special illumination from God concerning religious matters. This enlightenment saved them from the darkness of evil that besets all non-Gnostics. Salvation was by way of this special knowledge, not by the way of the cross. Christ did not suffer; it was Simon of Cyrene who died on the cross according to Valentinus, leader of the Roman Gnostics of Marcion's time.

This strange collection of ideas from Persia, Greece, and Rome provided the background for St. Justin's opposition to Gnostic thought. The first great attempt at a theology of Christ (Christology) was St. Irenaeus' defense of the faith against both Docetists and Gnostics called *"Against Heresies."*

IRENAEUS   Using Justin's idea of a word of God spoken partially in all creation, and finally spoken fully in the Word made flesh, Irenaeus centered his teaching on the theme of the Second Adam in whom all things are recapitulated—a Pauline idea (Eph 1,10–11) which Irenaeus developed beautifully. In Christ—"one and the same God and man" (his favorite expression, later used at Chalcedon)—the original divine plan for men was restored after Adam's shattering fall. The Second Adam recreated the whole human race by becoming one of us, thereby renovating all human history and life. No secret *gnōsis* accomplishes this salvation for men. Only the faith of the universal, apostolic Church in Christ can set them free. God's Word descended to earth so that with him we could ascend to heaven, become once more the image of God. Here is Irenaeus writing against pre-Arians:

> . . . he became a man liable to suffering; all the objections of those who say, "If our Lord was born at a certain time, Christ therefore had no previous existence," are set aside. For we have shown that the Son of God did not begin to exist then, since he existed with the Father from the beginning; but when he became incarnate and was made man, he recapitulated (summed up) in himself the long line of the human race, procuring for us salvation thus summarily; so that what we had lost in Adam—that is, being created in the image and likeness of God—we might regain in Christ Jesus. (*Against Heresies,* 3,18,1)

An outstanding theme which this bishop of Lyons developed was the sanctification of all stages of human life accomplished by Christ's living them. "He came to save all through his own person; all, that is, who through him are reborn to God: infants, children, boys, young men and old. Therefore he passed through every stage of life." (*Ibid.,* 2,22,4)

For Irenaeus, Christ was the focal point of creation and history, the mediator re-establishing peace between God and man because he "accustomed" God to man and vice versa. (*Ibid.,* 3,20,2) There is no question about the unity of God and man in Jesus Christ—Irenaeus would not abide the Gnostic distinction between Jesus the man and Christ the supernatural aeon.

> For it is not true that Christ then [at the baptism] descended on Jesus; nor are the Christ and Jesus two distinct persons, but the Word of God, the Savior of all and the ruler of heaven and earth, *is* Jesus. He took flesh; he was anointed by the Father with the Spirit and became Jesus Christ. . . . (*Ibid.,* 3,9,3)

This is Christology as we are accustomed to find it, but even in Irenaeus there are expressions vague enough to make us wonder exactly what he held. For him, the rational soul (*pneûma*) of Christ was not of primary importance. He probably first used the word "incarnation" (Greek: *ensárchōsis*) to describe the descent of the Word into humankind, as John's gospel had described it in 1,14. For anyone who would interpret "flesh" as mere corporeality, this would seem to deprive Christ of a human soul.

Another questionable idea of his (*Ibid.,* 3,19,3) was that in the miracles of Jesus the Word elevated the human nature to perform the wonders, whereas in the sufferings of Christ the Word remained quiescent. Danger of monenergism lurked in such a distinction, for it seemed to leave all real initiative to the godhead and the humanity relatively passive. But Irenaeus's great contributions to Christology far outweigh such vagueness, and we gladly remember him for inspiring passages such as this:

72

. . . there is only one Lord Jesus Christ who appeared throughout the universal economy of salvation and recapitulates in himself all things. In this totality man, the image of God, is included. Thus he recapitulates man in himself, the invisible becoming visible, the incomprehensible becoming comprehensible, the impassible becoming passible, the Word becoming man, gathering together all things in himself. As a result, just as the Word of God is supreme in the supra-celestial, spiritual and invisible world, so he has supremacy in the visible and corporeal world, and assumes in himself the primacy; while he places himself at the head of the church, he draws all things to himself in due time. (*Ibid.*, 3,16,6)

TERTULLIAN   Irenaeus wrote in Greek, since he came from the East. The Latin terminology of the Church was formed by the brilliant and tragic African convert, Tertullian, who eventually left the Church and died a Gnostic Montanist of rigoristic views on morality. In his orthodox days, however, his lawyer's mind keenly defended the Church's doctrine about the unity and duality of Christ against Marcion and other Docetists. He spoke of a "*duplex status*" of the Incarnate Word, using the Latin words "*substantia . . . natura*" to express each of the two realities in Christ, and the word "*persona*" to express his unity, thus anticipating Chalcedon's formula. (Cf. *Against Marcion*, 2,5; *Against Praxeas*, 27.)

Thus the quality of the two modes of being displayed both the humanity and the divinity: born as man, unborn as God; in one respect carnal, in the other spiritual; in one respect weak, in the other strong beyond measure; in one respect dying, in the other living. The proper qualities of the two conditions, the divine and the human, are attested by the equal reality of both natures: with the same faith the Spirit and the flesh are distinguished; the works of power attest the Spirit of God; the sufferings, the flesh of man. . . . If the flesh with its sufferings was a figment, then the Spirit with its mighty works was unreal. Why do you cut Christ in half with a lie? (*On the Flesh of Christ*, 5)

In this section, too, he stated the famous Christian paradox: "The Son of God died; one must believe it because it is absurd. He was buried and rose again; it is impossible, and therefore certain." (*Ibid.*) The mystery of Christ, accepted on faith, becomes its own guarantee.

One unusual notion of Tertullian that has not reappeared often in Christian history was that Christ was physically ugly. (*On the Flesh of Christ*, 9) He was much closer to our ideas in his defense of the true motherhood of Mary against Valentinus' contention that the Word merely passed through her like water through a channel. (*Ibid.*, 1; 17; 23) We catch a glimpse of the tough-minded courtroom orator in a passage such as the next, against Marcion the Docetist and his arbitrary denials of the evidence of the Church's book:

Clearly enough is the nativity announced by Gabriel. But what has he [Marcion] to do with the Creator's angel? . . . He will not brook delay, since suddenly, without any prophetic announcement he brings Christ down from heaven. "Away," says he, "with that eternal plaguey taxing of Caesar, and the scanty inn, and the squalid swaddling-clothes and the hard stable. . . ." In such a way as this, O Marcion, I suppose you have had the gall to blot out the original records of the history of Christ, that his flesh may lose the proofs of its reality. But tell me, on what grounds do you do this? Show me your authority. If you are a prophet, foretell us something. If you are an apostle, open your message in public. If you are a follower of the apostles, side with them in thought. If you are only an ordinary Christian, believe what has been handed down to us. But if you are none of these, then—as I have every good reason to say—drop dead! (*Ibid.,* 2)

Such forthrightness is refreshing in anyone when he is defending justice and truth as Tertullian was. His point was that Marcion was already dead in spirit because of his heretical teachings. Tertullian's own speculations about the manner of the incarnation were surprisingly orthodox and penetrating. He clearly saw that it could not be by any transformation of the eternal Word into something called man or even a God-man; then the unchanging God would have changed, and the third thing resulting would have been neither God nor man. (*Against Praxeas,* 27) He opted for the Word's being "clothed" with flesh, rather than being transformed into it; this clothing he explained as "coming to be in flesh" so that he became manifest and was seen as truly man. And this is orthodox enough.

CHRISTOLOGY'S TERMINOLOGY

Latin Usage

In the Latin-speaking West, therefore, Christology's terminology from Tertullian on was fairly well set, and passed through Augustine and Jerome to Leo I's famous Tome. (Cf. Chapter Eight.) The word *"persona"* (person) meant that which is one in Christ and three in the Trinity; the word *"natura . . . substantia,"* later *"essentia,"* meant that which is dual in Christ and one in the Trinity. Thus the West.

Interpretation in the East

In the East, however, two of the great cities and apostolic foundations had developed quite distinctive and diverse traditions of Bible interpretation. These led to difficulties when it came to agreeing on a terminology for the mystery of Christ.

74   ANTIOCH   At Antioch in Syria, the approach to the Bible was literal and rationalistic: what does the text *say?* Men of this tradition began with

Christ's humanness, the historical Jesus of Nazareth, and worked up to his divinity, the eternal Word. Such theorizing is not harmful if guided by the Church, but it is dangerous if, in this process, the humanity of Jesus comes to be the only reality of his earthly life. His divinity then runs the risk of being doubted or even denied.

Unfortunately, this is just what happened. Paul of Samosata, bishop of Antioch, began to teach that Christ was a mere man like the rest of us, except that God gave him a special spiritual power to do Godlike works. Christ, therefore, was not God, but was the minister of God, a specially adopted son in whom the Spirit of God dwelt as in a temple, making him *"homooúsios"* with God—that is, manifesting the same spiritual power as God. A Synod of Antioch quickly declared such teaching erroneous, and deposed the bishop in 268 A.D. Paul's catchword, *homooúsios,* was temporarily relegated to the theological scrapheap. It would be rescued from there by the Council of Nicea in 325 A.D., which would refurbish it by giving it a new meaning; forever it lies gleaming in the creed of that council in the sense of "consubstantial."

Antioch's stress on Christ's humanity may well be what modern Catholics need in order to have an integral appreciation of the incarnation of the Son of God and a deep understanding of the New Testament. Some modern Protestants seem to be neo-Nestorians who go too far in the direction of emphasis on Christ's humanity. By the same token, too many Catholics are so engrossed in the divinity of Christ as to deny his full status as man.

ALEXANDRIA   At Alexandria in Egypt, another great tradition took shape in a catechetical school founded about 190 A.D. This was the city where the Septuagint had been translated, and where Philo had tried to combine Judaism with Hellenic philosophy. The intellectual tradition of this city was established. Its neo-Platonic philosophy influenced the Christian approach to Scripture, producing a primary interest in the *meaning* of Jesus rather than in Antioch's historical Son of Mary. The spiritual interpretation of the New Testament was the focal point of study; to draw out the religious and moral meanings of the text, the question was asked, What does the text *mean?*

Beginning with the Word's pre-existence and divinity, the Alexandrian school worked down to Christ's humanity, the Word made flesh. Once again, the only serious danger lay in understressing the full humanness of Christ, with the consequent temptation to Docetism or, later, Monophysitism. Modern Catholics often seem more inclined to this Alexandrian imbalance than to the Antiochene one.

Clement of Alexandria.   But to return to religious history. Clement of Alexandria was the first great theologian of this school, though his writings are often more interesting for their insights into daily life—how to use a toothpick, and where—than for their theological richness. The personal belief of this "Christian Gnostic" was unlike that of most other forms of Gnosticism. For him, simple faith develops into a deep and penetrating knowledge

75

(*gnōsis*) which then is perfected in the heavenly vision of God. Clement's *gnōsis* seems to have been something like the theological wisdom of a saint like John of the Cross or Thomas Aquinas, a desirable *gnōsis* indeed.

His Christology, however, left much to be desired. Stressing the transcendence of the *Lógos* (Word), Clement seemed to say that Christ's body was attached to the Word in such a way as to be directed by it without reciprocally affecting the Word by any of its bodily weaknesses. Of the rational soul he says little or nothing. His interest is in maintaining the utter spiritual perfection of the Word, which he placed in a kind of Stoic "apathy." In other words the Word was completely superior to anything like bodily emotions or experiences. Thus, Clement could write:

> But in the case of the Savior it would be absurd to suppose that his body demanded the essential services for his stay. For he ate, not because of bodily needs, since his body was supported by holy power, but so that his companions might not entertain a false notion about him, as in fact certain men did later, namely that he had been manifested only in appearance. He himself was, and remained, "untroubled by passion"; no movement of the passions, either pleasure or pain, found its way into him. (*Miscellanies*, 6,9,71)

This does not sound like orthodoxy. The spiritual interpretation of Scripture lay open to this danger. Lest Clement seem to have spoken always this way, here he is in one of his better moments. "This Word, the Christ, the cause of our being . . . as also of our wellbeing, has now appeared to man. He alone is both God and man." (*Exhortation to the Greeks*, 1,7) "Believe, O man, in him who is man and God; believe in him who suffered and is worshipped as the living God. Servants, believe in him who was dead; all men, believe in him who is the only God of all men." (*Ibid.*, 10,106) ". . . the Word of God, who became man precisely that you may learn from a man how it may be that man should become God." (*Ibid.*, 1,8,4) His words are biblical rather than theological, as he reflects a time when the living tradition of the Church was being committed to nonbiblical writing more and more. The Church's rule of faith was all the while guiding the expression of Christian mysteries. Clement was much less important in the development of Christology in the East, however, than was Origen, an equally complex individual.

Origen. This amazing man was the glory of his school (first Alexandria, then Caesarea in Palestine), and one of the all-time greats in the Church. Not even some misguided opinions and even more misguided disciples, who later brought suspicion upon his name, can veil this fact. His learning was massive, his interests universal, his curiosity insatiable. Origen attempted a complete system of theology; he was the first so to do, and was fortunate in crowning his life's work by dying for Christ in 252 A.D. as a result of maltreatment during the persecution of Decius. Like Clement, he was a

Christian Gnostic. He believed that the allegorical meaning of Scripture was the truest, and known only to the masters of interpretation. Ironically, his interpretation of Mt 19,12 was one of the most literal recorded.

Origen's Christology is basically sound, despite his tendency to subordinationism in trinitarian theology. Often enough he is perfectly clear about the eternity of the Son, as in his great work, *On the Principles of Things,* 1,2,2. The quality of his Christian faith is evident in wonderful passages like this:

> But of all the marvellous and mighty acts related of him, this altogether surpasses human admiration, and is beyond the power of mortal frailty to understand or feel, how that mighty power of divine majesty, that very Word of the Father, and that very wisdom of God in which were created all things, visible and invisible, can be believed to have existed within the limits of that man who appeared in Judea. More, that the wisdom of God can have entered the womb of a woman, and have been born an infant, and have uttered wailings like the cries of little children! . . . Since, then, we see in him some things so human that they appear to differ in no respect from the common frailty of mortals, and some things so divine that they can appropriately belong to nothing else than to the primal and ineffable nature of deity, the narrowness of human understanding can find no outlet. . . . Therefore the spectacle is to be contemplated with all fear and reverence, that the truth of both natures may be clearly shown to exist in one and the same being; so that nothing unworthy or unbecoming may be perceived in that divine and ineffable substance, nor yet those things which were done be supposed to be the illusions of imaginary appearances. (*Ibid.,* 2,6,2)

As is evident Origen is no Docetist, yet for him Christ's body had an ethereal quality which enabled it to change as and when he willed. (*Against Celsus* 3,41) The rational soul of Christ enabled the Word to become flesh, mediating between the spiritual God and the corporeal body to make contact of the two possible. His soul was like ours, except that no sin or sinfulness could touch him; for him, it was second nature to be and to do good. (*On the Principles,* 2,6,5) His soul was immersed in God like iron in a fire that seems to become the fire itself. (*Ibid.,* 2,6,6)

Origen was first to use the term "God-man"—*theánthrōpos,* in Greek. He clearly described the paradoxical fact known as the "interchange of properties" between the divinity and the humanity of Christ.

> The Son of God, through whom all things were created, is called Jesus Christ and the son of man. For the Son of God is said to have died with respect to that nature which was certainly capable of death; and he is called the Son of Man who is proclaimed about to come in the glory of the Father with the holy angels. For this reason throughout the whole of scripture, the divine nature is spoken of in human

77

terms, and at the same time the human nature is accorded the distinctive epithets proper to the divine. For the saying, "The two shall be in one flesh, and they are now not two but one flesh," is more applicable here than in any other reference. (*Ibid.*, 2,6,3)

For Origen, the process of the Word's descent was better termed "humanization" (Greek: *enanthrōpēsis*) than "incarnation." This was most likely an improvement on what seemed to be an identification of humanity with mere flesh. The correlative danger, though, was to consider Christ's humanity as that of a pre-existing man brought into union with the Word—the *"assumptus homo"* of twelfth-century theories.

In his manner of explaining the mystery, Origen was necessarily unsure at this stage of the Church's theology. He said there were two realities (Greek: *ousíai*) in Christ and a unity (Greek: *hénōsis*, not merely a *koinōnía*, a sharing) which he sometimes called a commingling (Greek: *anákrasis*) as in *Against Celsus*, 3,28. At times he termed Christ a composite thing (Greek: *sýntheton chrēma*) but simultaneously one thing, because the Word united himself far more perfectly with this human soul in divine love than with any prophet or apostle. (*On the Principles*, 2,6,4) This sounds like a merely moral union, of course, so we cannot be sure of his final opinion.

Of this we can be sure, though. Origen made possible the work of the fathers of Nicea, of St. Athanasius, champion of its formula, and of the orthodox Cappadocian theologians who followed him. Arius claimed to be his disciple, but unjustly. Athanasius is the true heir of Origen. He profited by his speculations but was also hindered by his ambiguous use of the Greek words: *phýsis, hypóstasis, ousía,* and *prósōpon*. Not until 433 A.D. were churchmen to agree on the proper use of these terms.

Our next chapter will relate this development in Christology.

CHAPTER EIGHT

CHRIST
IN THE COUNCILS
CHRISTOLOGICAL

Is Christ one "thing" or two? One "being" or two? Or should the question be: *has* he one "being" or two? The latter topic will be taken up in the next chapter; this one will consider the slow, tortuous development of the Church's expression of her faith in the Word made flesh, until she definitively declared: He is one person with two natures. That is, he is one "Thing," and two "things." Obviously, then, the words must be carefully used; careless use of them occasioned bloodshed in the past, as we shall see.

The challenge of stating in human terms the data of supernatural revelation is illustrated well in the history of Christology in the councils of the Church. Everyone was reading the same Scriptures; everyone wanted to express the same faith; not everyone was willing to accept formulations other than his own. Before the Council of Chalcedon in 451 A.D., this diversity in word usage was understandable and excusable; after Chalcedon's "one person with two natures," any diversity was heresy. Salvation, then, was at stake in this controversy, and still is.

Barriers to Unity of Belief

Many circumstances led to the posing of the problem and the importance of how it was posed. One significant influence was the distance that separated Rome from Constantinople—a couple of jet-hours away now, but a journey of several months by slow boat then. Messages and messengers exhausted half a year getting back and forth, so that delays, misunderstandings of terms used, even deaths of the people concerned, were ordinary factors in the development of Christology during the first centuries of the Church. Politics, too, played its part. Constantine had divided the Roman world into East and West, with an Imperator cogoverning in each. Well-meaning as he may have been, he introduced the civil power into the sanctuary. Its influence has occasionally been of benefit there, but far more often it has resulted in trouble, embarrassment, and even tragedy for Christianity.

A third major influence was the differing attitude toward the study of Christ current in the two then most prominent Christian schools, one at Alexandria (Egypt), the other at Antioch (Syria). As we saw in Chapter Seven, the first emphasized his divinity. It began with his godhead, worried about his humanness later, and in general was struck with awe at the wonder of *God's* becoming man. The second emphasized his humanity. It began with his humanness, reached his godhead later, and in general was struck with wonder at this *man's* claim to equal status with God. The two attitudes are by no means contradictory. No doubt each of us believers has a bit of Alexandria and a bit of Antioch in him. But historically, these diverse attitudes toward Christ and his story led to bitter disputes. In reading Scripture, Alexandria tended first to see spiritual meaning in all the events of our Lord's life. Antioch on the other hand tended to seek first only what humanly happened.

The political, economic, and cultural rivalry of these two great Eastern sees added to the intensity of their competition, as each brought all possible pressure to bear on Constantinople, the imperial city soon to be declared the "second Rome." Into these ingredients stir the personalities of Arius, Nestorius, Cyril, Pope Leo, Emperor Theodosius, and the others, and all the elements for high drama are present. This is a brief sketch of that dramatic history.

Arius

Arius, a priest of Alexandria, may be taken as a starting point for this part of the story. To him, the phrase "the Word became flesh" meant just that, if flesh is understood to mean corporeality in the Hellenistic sense and not complete "humanity" in the Semitic. Arius seems far more Antiochene than Alexandrian in his approach, at least to this phrase. For him, a "man" is a soul inhabiting a body and giving life to it—a neo-Platonic conception of human nature. The flesh of Christ was a mere lifeless body with no soul animating it until the Word of God (who was *not* God himself but was the highest creature ever made), supplied life to that inanimate flesh. Christ was the needed mediator between the invisible, spiritual God and the visible creation; he was the Word (Greek: *Lógos*) spoken into the world, the Word through which the world was made; but he was not God.

Athanasius

St. Athanasius, also a priest of Alexandria (he had accompanied Bishop Alexander to Nicaea as his secretary, but there is no record of his activity at the council), set the general tone for the truly Christian answer to all heretics. He maintained that what Christ did not assume, he did not redeem. If Christ did not take to himself our complete humanness, then we are not completely redeemed. Therefore *he became whatever we are,* that is, "man." The Word was made flesh, or became man, as the readers of St. John well knew from the context of his gospel and epistles.

Nicaea

The Council of Nicaea met in 325 A.D. at Constantine's bidding but with the legates of the Roman See—chiefly Bishop Ossius of Cordoba (Spain) —presiding. It declared Arius to be wrong on two counts at least. Christ the Son was defined to be God in the same sense as the Father is, "the same thing as God is." In Greek the term employed was *"homooúsios,"* translated into Latin as "consubstantialis." We sing or say this at Mass, where the Creed is that of Nicaea-Constantinople; we publicly declare with the bishops of Nicaea that the Lord Jesus is what God is. We also use the council's words about the incarnation: he was made flesh—he became man.

The word *homooúsios* became the touchstone of Christianity subsequent to Nicaea, distinguishing the loyal from the rebels. There had been a time when to espouse it meant that one had Sabellian leanings. Now, because of the Council's use of *homooúsios*, to reject it meant rejecting the full divinity of Christ. The Greek word *"ousía"* was used in 325 to mean "what God the Father is" and later by extension, "what God is." In 381 the first Council of

Constantinople declared that the same is true of God's Spirit, namely that he is what God the Father and God the Son are.

This decision settled the trinitarian matter of whether Christ is God or not, or rather settled it by reaffirming the Church's faith and declaring that Arius's teaching did not accord with that faith. It did not solve the Christological problem of whether and how the divinity is united to full humanity. Christ is a divine "thing" just as much as the Father is. Is he also a human "thing" like us or is he missing something—something perhaps that makes us human? If not, is he then two things rather than one? If two, are they united somehow? These are the properly Christological problems.

Apollinaris

Apollinaris, bishop of Laodicea, strenuously fought Arianism's denial of a human soul to Jesus Christ, but in so doing fell into an error of his own that subsequently led generations of Christians to lose the sense of the full humanity of our Lord. His point against Arius was that the Word took to himself not mere lifeless flesh, but rather an animated human body. His error was in supposing that this body was animated only by a vegetative-animal soul, all intellectual activity stemming from the Word himself. This, he thought, would ensure that all Christ's thoughts would be God's thoughts, so that no danger of conflicting views would exist in him. Christ would then be sure to redeem us in spite of the prospective pain of the passion; all chance that he might shrink and turn back had been eliminated, in this view. Apollinaris used the term "one *phýsis*" to express the unique *thing* that the Word incarnate is. Note this word well: *phýsis* (plural: *phýseis*). In the Greek usage of the time, it meant what we would term "the total reality" of a thing. But note, it also *could* mean "the real source of activity" of a thing—and thereby hung many a tale of heresy.

Take the teaching of Apollinaris as an example. In saying that the Word incarnate is one *phýsis,* he could mean it in the orthodox sense of "a unified and united reality." But he also could mean that the eternal Word was the "only real source of activity" in Christ, and thereby deny something truly human about him. He chose to deny true human, intellectual activity in denying a human mind to our Lord. Later, St. Gregory of Nazianz would wryly remark that whoever places his hope in a mindless man, is missing a mind himself! (M. J. Rouet de Journel, *Enchiridion Patristicum,* 17th ed. [Freiburg: Herder, 1951], 1018.)

Local synods of bishops in both Alexandria and Rome (377 A.D.) condemned Apollinaris' dehumanization of Christ, and Pope Damasus anathematized

. . . those who say that in the human body [of Christ] the Word of God dwelt in place of the rational and intellective human soul; because the very Son and Word of God did not take the place of the rational and intellective soul in his body, but he assumed and preserved a soul like ours . . . but without sin. (*TCT*, No. 397, p. 166)

From now on, to say "one *phýsis*" of Christ had to mean "one concrete unified reality" and not "one only source of activity," in the sense that only the Word acted in Christ. No, human thoughts had to be ascribed to Christ, stemming from a human soul which was the source of all kinds of properly human activity. The next heretic we encounter gladly seized on this.

Nestorius

Nestorius, schooled at Antioch and in 428 made bishop of Constantinople, is that man. Just as Arius is forever famous for denying "*homooúsios*," this cleric remains in Christian minds as the one who denied that Mary is the bearer of God, in Greek, "*theotókos*." He was perfectly willing to acknowledge her as mother of "the man Christ," or of the sacred humanity of God, but not of God himself. How any creature could give birth to the eternal One who made her was Nestorius' problem. She is not "*theotókos*," therefore, but at most "*Christotókos*"—the woman who bore the man Jesus Christ.

This denial of Mary's motherhood of the divine underlines Nestorius' overemphasis on the humanness of the Word incarnate. Christ is so human that his humanity exists and acts on its own, independently of and separately from his godhead. He is *a man,* in every respect like us—sin alone excepted. He is also God, of course, for the Nicene creed says he is what God is. Nestorius probably at first thought that he was only saying that Christ is also *what we humans are,* but his denial of *theotókos* showed that his idea of Christ's real unity was defective. For him Christ was two things, and each thing (*phýsis*) was complete in itself, existing by itself but in combination, somehow, in the one Christ. He was two individuals acting as one. The Nestorian error accounts for the favored usage in Catholic writing which speaks of Christ as "man," not as "a man." The latter is occasionally seen in Catholic writing and is of course a shortened form of "a-divine-person-who-is-man." Nonetheless, the reader should know why some resist this usage vigorously.

Nestorius held, then, that Christ was made up of two "*phýseis*" but that these two coexisted peacefully and cooperatively. In him, only the eternal Word was true God; the human *phýsis* was distinct and also independent in its existence. His error was that Christ was God and *a* man simultaneously, not one united God-man, eternal Son of the Father and Mary's son in time. When questioned about his theory of the unity of Christ, Nestorius could not give a clear explanation. He used examples such as that of God indwelling in Christ's humanity as in a temple, or the unity of husband and wife in one flesh. Perhaps we have something similar in our use of the title, "*Mr. and Mrs.* John Smith," to designate two humans by a common name. Another possible comparison would be a Christian receiving holy communion: when

83

the Word dwells within him he is a God-bearer, *Christophóros* if not *Christotókos*. This would be a type of physical unity with Christ, but one that leaves the communicant free and independent of the God within him. Clearly he is not one thing with God, and is only so united for a short time.

At times Nestorius seemed to mean that Christ's union with the Word was only a matter of conforming his human will perfectly to the divine will, as Mary did. This would make him the greatest saint ever, but again, not God.

Cyril of Alexandria

Cyril, bishop of Alexandria and later a saint, opposed these innovations of his opposite number in Constantinople, especially the denial of *theotókos*. Being trained in the Egyptian school, he stressed the pre-existent Word, as Paul and John had done. This one infinite Son of God became also the son of Mary.

> Confessing then that the Word was united hypostatically [in a real, personal union] to flesh, we worship one Son and Lord Jesus Christ, neither separating—dividing man and God as though they had been joined in a union of dignity or authority, for this would be empty words and nothingness—nor again describing the Word of God, "Christ," separately from the one [born] of a woman, another "christ"; but knowing only one Christ, the Word of God the Father, with his own flesh. . . . Since the holy Virgin brought forth by human generation God, personally united to flesh, we say that she is Theotokos: not as though the nature of the Word had the beginning of its existence from flesh—for he "was in the beginning," and "the Word was God"—but . . . since he personally united manhood to himself he also underwent a fleshly birth from her womb, not that he needed begetting in time either necessarily or on account of his own nature [*phýsis*] . . . but that he might bless the very beginning of our existence. . . ." (Cyril's Third Letter to Nestorius)

Cyril stressed the *unity* of the Word incarnate, and he adopted as one of his rallying-cries: "One *phýsis* of God the Word incarnate." By *phýsis* he had in mind the general meaning of the word: one total concrete reality; he sometimes used the word *"hypóstasis"* in the same way. St. Cyril's use of the terms was orthodox, as the second Council of Constantinople was to declare in 553 A.D. But the formula, which he thought came from St. Athanasius, was actually one used by Apollinaris, and could be so misinterpreted that it would seem to deny any reality to the humanness of Christ. The heretic Eutyches did just this, twenty years later.

Cyril, however, was opposing Nestorius' exaggeration of the human element in our Lord. He was making sure that Christians believed that the child in the manger was the eternal Son of God, not some hybrid combination of God and man which would destroy the reality of our redemption. There was

84

one integral reality which included both God the Word and the child; there was one *phýsis* of the Word incarnate.

EPHESUS

The Council

His use of this word *phýsis*, however, confused more people than Nestorius. Some thought he meant "the real source of activity" of a being, and consequently understood him to be denying any real human activity in Christ. John, bishop of Antioch, was one of these. When a Council was called for Ephesus in 431 A.D. to deal with Nestorius, he set out for the city with his followers, determined to teach Cyril and the Alexandrians the proper use of terms, whether or not Nestorius was orthodox. To his surprise, he found on his arrival that the Council had already been opened, Nestorius condemned, and Cyril hailed as the defender of the Christian faith. He understandably became very angry.

What had happened was this. Cyril had tried for months to get Nestorius to admit his error in dividing Christ into two: God and a man. Failing in this, he had written to Pope Celestine in Rome; so had Nestorius, in defense of his own side of the issue. Celestine had written to both of them declaring Cyril to be in the right and demanding a retractation from Nestorius of this ". . . innovation, which aims as separating what the venerable Scripture has joined together." (Quoted in *Lux Veritatis*, NCWC translation, p. 10) The pope deputed Cyril to see to it that Nestorius so retracted, but even before his letter arrived in the East, Emperor Theodosius II had convoked a council for June 7, 431, to clear up the question in the Eastern Church. Hearing of this, Pope Celestine agreed to it and sent legates to preside. But before they arrived, and after waiting two weeks past the date set, Cyril opened the council. On June 22 he had Nestorius condemned on the charge of having denied the Nicene Creed. John of Antioch and his bishops arrived on June 24 to find the council apparently over. He promptly appealed to the Emperor and went into session with his own followers, proclaiming solemnly that Cyril was a heretic like Apollinaris, and had forfeited his see.

The arrival of the papal legates fortunately intervened. To John's disgust, they confirmed the June 22 session and judged the condemnation of Nestorius valid. His teaching was contrary to the Nicene Creed, to Pope Celestine's letter to the council, and to Cyril's letters to him. The Antiochene session of John and his group was declared out of order. They were ordered to appear before the council, and upon failing to appear, were summarily excommunicated. The Emperor now decided to get into the matter and ordered the arrest of the disputing leaders: Nestorius, Bishop Memnon of Ephesus, and Cyril himself. Eventually the Emperor consented to the deposition of Nestorius alone, but it took a good deal of ecclesiastical politicking by Cyril to make sure of the triumph of orthodoxy. God's ways are obviously not our ways, and Cyril's activities at court in securing the condemnation of Nestorius have found justification (cf. *Lux Veritatis,* p. 17) in light of the orthodox outcome of the affair.

Formula of Union

John of Antioch went home angry, but since both men desired peace in the Church they worked out a mutually agreeable formula through letters exchanged during the next year and more. In 433 they agreed on what is known as the Formula of Union, in which John's terminology was combined with Cyril's. The crucial word *phýsis* is used for each of the realities united, divinity and humanity, and Cyril's earlier "one *phýsis*" formula was relegated to the ashheap of controversy—they hoped. Christ's unity was expressed in the Greek word *"prósōpon,"* which in Latin is *"persona"* and in English "person." Christ is now termed one person with two *phýseis*—two "natures," as we now can term them. He is one "Thing," but he is also two things. In the Ephesine words, he is "one (person) from two things," *unus ex duobus;* and Mary is *Theotókos,* truly mother of the one true God. To quote Cyril again:

> That the Word was made flesh means that He had a share like us of flesh and blood. He made our body His own and came forth as man from a woman, not losing divinity nor origin from the Father, but in assuming flesh remained what He was. (*Ibid.,* p. 20)

The matter seemed to be settled at last, and the terms agreed on: Christ was one person with two natures. He was one Christ, one Son, one Lord, consubstantial with the Father in his divinity and consubstantial with us in his humanity. Let the Church get on with the conversion of the pagan nations, even now on the move across Europe and Asia Minor.

CHALCEDON

Monophysitism

But no, God's providence did not work that way. Cyril's Apollinarian formula "one *phýsis* of the incarnate Word" now came back to haunt the peacemakers. Over in Alexandria the bishop was Dioscorus, onetime deacon of Cyril and therefore convinced that he knew the mind of his great master as no one else did. Dioscorus heard they were saying "two natures" now and claiming this as Cyril's doctrine, whereas he well knew the "one nature" battlecry against Nestorius. In Constantinople there presided bishop Flavian, imbued with this "old error," an insult to the memory of Cyril and the fathers of Ephesus. When an old monk named Eutyches, who was head of a huge monastery outside Constantinople, appealed to Cyril's formula against the Formula of Union of 433 (equally Cyril's formula, of course), Dioscorus was only too eager to back him up. They both claimed to be defending the Church against a new Nestorianism. Eutyches was godfather to Chrysaphius, chief minister of Emperor Theodosius; this meant that he had a strong ally at court in days when such allies were the necessary protection for being right—or at least being temporarily victorious—in controversy religious. Pope Leo I later said that Eutyches was not too intelligent a man; his ascetic life, spread over ninety years, had perhaps dimmed his theological wisdom a bit, too. At any rate, he was attacking Nestorianism in Cyril's name.

Eutyches' theory was to become known as Monophysitism, the heresy that there is only one *nature* in Christ. Verbally, it is Cyril's formula, of course. After 433 it was not really Cyril's thought at all, for he had agreed to use the word *phýsis* for *each* of the two realities in the incarnate Word. The old man, though, was touchingly faithful to what he thought Cyril meant, and Dioscorus backed him up when he needed backing.

Flavian

This was in 448, when a local bishop accused Eutyches of heresy at a synod in Constantinople. Bishop Flavian summoned the aged monk, who refused to admit two *phýseis* in Christ despite their explaining to him the differences in Cyril's use of the terms. The synod deposed him from office, as a heretic.

Monophysitism of Eutyches' brand holds that, after the union, only one nature remained in the incarnate Word. Before union, two natures existed. Mary gave the Word a human body, but the human nature was "absorbed" in the divine reality in such a way that really only the divinity was left after union. It was as if a bottle of wine had absorbed a drop of water so that it was no longer perceptible in the liquid, or to use Eutyches' figure, a drop of honey had been received into the ocean.

Centuries later, Pope Pius XII would remark in his encyclical *Sempiternus Rex,* on the fifteenth centenary of Chalcedon, that Eutyches' theory was baseless on several counts. First, the human nature did not exist before the union, so could hardly be absorbed into anything. Second, the divine nature had always existed in the Son, infinite in its reality and susceptible of no change, so that it surely could not be combined with anything and be changed into a third thing. Eutyches imagined the change somewhat as hydrogen and oxygen are combined to form water. But this is impossible in the case of the Son's infinitely perfect and eternal person. The ancient monk appealed to Rome in anti-Nestorian terms, enjoying the Emperor's firm support and Chrysaphius' assurance of pressure in the right places. Bishop Flavian also wrote, and drew from Pope Leo I the great document known as *Tomus Leonis* ("Pope Leo's Tome"), a letter to Flavian about the incarnation which has remained normative in doctrine and devotion ever since.

Robber Synod

This *Tome* did not arrive, however, until after Emperor Theodosius had called a local council in Ephesus in 449, where Dioscorus of Alexandria presided and Monophysitism was hailed as the faith of the Church. It was an incredible and tragic meeting of violent men intent on having their way. They deposed Flavian as a Nestorian who would not accept Cyril's first formula. He was so ill-treated, probably by Dioscorus himself, that he died three days later. On hearing what had taken place, Pope Leo branded this council *Latrocinium,* and the name has stuck: the Council of Robbers—the Mafia of their day.

The victims of this brigandage appealed to Rome, of course, and Leo acted. His Tome had already been sent and it was now in the hands of authorities in Constantinople. He protested to the emperor, asking him to convoke a truly ecumenical council somewhere in Italy and at once. Theodosius brushed off the request. Leo had the Western Imperator, Valentinian III, make the same petition, but Theodosius refused even this, with the cynical remark that all was peaceful on his side of the world. Just when a permanent split within the Eastern Church seemed inevitable, death intervened. Theodosius ended his days through an accident on his horse, and on July 28, 450, his sister Pulcheria succeeded to the throne. Eutyches' patron, Chrysaphius, was executed at once. Pulcheria appealed to Rome for a council, and Pope Leo gladly agreed to have it at Chalcedon, just across the Bosporus from Constantinople. It met in 451 and is the great Christological council.

Leo

Leo wrote a second letter now, insisting that the council approve his previous Tome. This was done by the six hundred bishops attending, with the papal legates presiding over them all. Leo's words and thoughts are still moving.

> Hence, the proper character of each nature was kept inviolate, and together they were united in one person. Thus was lowliness assumed by majesty, weakness by power, mortality by eternity; a nature that could not be defiled was united to one that could suffer in order to repay the debt attaching to our state. . . . In the full and perfect nature of true man, therefore, the true God was born. . . . And so the Son of God, descending from his heavenly throne, yet not leaving the glory of the Father, enters into this world's weakness and is generated in a new manner, born with a new birth. . . . Yet the miraculous manner of our Lord Jesus Christ's birth, born as he was from the womb of a virgin, does not make his nature any different from ours. For the same person is true God and true man; and there is no deception in this unity in which the lowliness of man and the dignity

of God are joined. For as God, he suffers no change because of his condescension, nor as man, is he absorbed by the divine dignity; for each nature performs the functions proper to itself, yet in conjunction with the other nature: the Word does what is proper to the Word, and the humanity what is proper to the humanity. (TCT412f, p. 171)

The Decree

The council then gave judgment against Monophysitism, deposed Dioscorus, and demoted Eutyches. On the new emperor's insistence, the bishops drew up a fresh declaration of faith which was supposed to settle permanently the terminological argument. They used Pope Leo's ideas and the Greek terms of the Formula of Union of 433. According to the framing of Chalcedon, Christ is perfect both in his divinity and in his humanity, consubstantial with the Father and also with us, truly son of Mary as he is truly Son of the Father.

> We declare that the one selfsame Christ, only-begotten Son and Lord, must be acknowledged in two natures [*phýseis*] without any commingling or change or division or separation; that the distinction between the natures [*phýseis*] is in no way removed by their union but rather that the specific character of each nature [*phýsis*] is preserved and they are united in one person [*prósōpon*] and one *hypóstasis*. We declare that he is not split or divided into two persons [*prósōpa*, plural] but that there is one selfsame only-begotten Son, God the Word, the Lord Jesus Christ. (TCT414, p. 172)

This was clear theological language at last, and settled much while leaving the mystery intact. Faith means some opaqueness in the object, after all. From then on, Christ was to be termed "one person (*prósōpon* or *hypóstatis*) with two natures (*phýseis* or *ousíai*)." He was one Thing, but also two things: divine and human, God and man. One complete and total reality, one autonomous and independent Son of God, he also was able to live and act as Son of Mary. Without this completeness he would not be what he really was: the Word incarnate. Our redemption was assured; he who died for us was God in human nature. This teaching was summed up at the second Council of Constantinople in 553. (TCT420, p. 176; D217. Cf. TCT418)

CONSTANTINOPLE III

One last large heresy remained to be raised, again in the East and again with political overtones. Monophysitism had not curled up and died after Chalcedon, but had taken whole districts of the Empire out of communion with Rome and Rome's Eastern bishops. This was a constant care to the empire, and one which the rulers wanted eased. One form of this heresy has become known as *Monothelitism* (Greek: *thelō*, I will) and held that there is only one will in Christ, the divine will, of course. As Apollinaris had feared the consequences of a human intellect in Christ, so these men dreaded the admission of a free human will in him, similarly lest our redemption be endangered. A Christ humanly free to disobey his Father's will might refuse to die on the cross, they reasoned, so his divine will must have "taken over" and done all the willing for him. This way, redemption was assured.

Redemption could have been assured that way, yes. But what of the actual way in which Christ accomplished it? What would the prayer of Christ in the garden, "Not my will but thine be done," mean? Could the infinite will of God be somehow diverse, distinct? Faith in the Trinity, coequal in power and majesty, dispelled that possibility; therefore Christ had to have some human reality in him that he termed his "will." At a Roman Synod in 649 A.D., Pope Martin I rejected any denial that Christ "has two wills harmoniously united, one divine and one human, inasmuch as he willed our salvation in a natural way through each of his natures." (*TCT*439, p. 183) The Third Ecumenical Council of Constantinople in 680–681 took up this Roman condemnation and declared Monothelitism a heresy. Imperial unity was not to be gained at Christ's expense. Redemption was assured not by the absorption of a human will into the divine, but by the subordination of the human will to the divine and the harmonious cooperation of the two. Human decisions and human choices belonged to Christ as results of human psychological processes. His emotions reacted to good-evil stimuli even as ours do, and his human will was fully free in its own sphere of activity. His human will was also fully united in perfect charity with the will of the Father, as our wills are not. His super-abundant personal grace as head of the human race was permanent and assured; he was certain to redeem us, his members. But more of this in the next chapter.

SUMMARY

A few words in summary and conclusion. If this chapter should seem to be a long quibble over words, and not much more, let us consider for a moment how important words are when they stand for things we hold most dear. Remember the life-and-death importance of the meaning of words like "Free city of Berlin . . . civil rights . . . academic freedom . . . democracy . . . peace." In the early centuries of the Church, men died or went into exile for the words that expressed their beliefs. What difference does it make, whether the Word is *homooúsios* or *homoioúsios* with the Father, Mary *Theotókos* or only *Christotókos*? For the Christian Church of history, it makes us all the difference in this world and the next. Each word is significant for us, too, since most of us are of that Church—indeed are that Church.

CHAPTER NINE

CHRIST IN THE THEOLOGIANS

To cover in one short chapter the developments in Christology from 681 A.D. to the present day is beyond the possibilities of this small volume. Aware of this fact, we shall at least realize that much is being omitted which might well be studied for deeper understanding or as the subject of a term paper. We shall be concerned with some theological reflections on the data of faith, largely drawn from St. Thomas Aquinas, and with some current suggestions for future lines of development. This chapter, then, should serve as an introduction to a modern theological rethinking of the mystery of the incarnate Word, for an increase of faith.

Ephesus and Chalcedon had left the Church's understanding of this mystery somewhat like this: Christ is the one, second person who from eternity exists as the unchanging Son of God, and who in time took a second nature to himself when he became son of Mary. He could not become another person, a second total reality, without ceasing to be perfect God—and this is manifestly impossible. Therefore his eternal act of being, which gave him infinite reality before the incarnation, continued to do so in his taking flesh and after it. His human nature, received from Mary, is (exists) because of a connection somehow with the eternal act of being-the-Son. This connection is due to the grace of union, the most wonderful and deifying grace possible for any creature. It makes the created nature belong to God personally as his own. God is man! And man is God.

The Church agreed in her great councils that the unifying principle in the God-man is his person (*hypóstasis*); the duality is expressed by the somewhat vague word, natures (*phýseis*). He is one Thing, but in him there are two realities. His humanity is just as real to him as his divinity, and as properly his own. Each is complete and total in its own way: he is not partly God nor is he partly human. The heretics usually wished to make a dilemma of him: either divine or human. The Church insisted on both-and, thereby preserving the full biblical revelation. "One and the same Jesus Christ is both God and man." Whatever is included in the idea and reality God, as well as in the idea and reality man, is true of Christ. *"E duobus unus"* would fairly describe the Christology of Catholics—one in two. The union is more intimate by an infinity, needless to say, in the Christian mystery than in the political reality.

ST. THOMAS AQUINAS

St. Thomas in the greatest of all his theological works, the *Summa Theologiae*, followed the order that he believed would best coordinate the data of the mysteries of our religion. In the First Part of the *Summa*, God is the subject—the one and triune God, creator and sanctifier of the world. In the two divisions of the Second Part, he wrote of man as a creature of God destined for loving union with him. The Third Part considers the unique God-man, summing up in himself all reality and joining man closely to God as the *Way* of salvation. This concluding part shows the heights to which humanity can be raised.

In following out this magnificent plan, St. Thomas inherited and used the treasures of the Church: St. Augustine's thought above all, but also that of St. John of Damascus in the East, the Franciscan Alexander of Hales, and Peter Lombard. The writings of these men were his textbooks as student and teacher. All theologians since his time are indebted to him, whether they have known it or not. All of us would profit from considering the central ideas of his theology of Christ in the Third Part of the *Summa*. The Church's judgment on his importance has been rendered again and again, notably by Pope Pius XII:

> . . . the Church demands that future priests be instructed in philosophy "according to the method, doctrine, and principles of the Angelic Doctor" [Code of Canon Law, 1366, No. 2] since, as we well know from the experience of centuries, the method of Aquinas is singularly pre-eminent both for teaching students and for bringing truth to light; his doctrine is in harmony with divine revelation, and is most effective both for safeguarding the foundation of the faith, and for reaping, safely and usefully, the fruits of sound progress. (*Humani Generis*, NCWC translation, No. 31)

St. Thomas's theological insights are surely no less recommended to other Catholics than to those who aspire to the priesthood. Without claiming for the following pages any definitive interpretation of the *Summa*, we hope to stay within the authentic tradition called Thomistic that has been graced by so many and diverse scholars.

Theology

In attempting to state the mystery of the incarnation in theological and not merely biblical terms, we must use philosophical principles. Theology as such is a penetration of the data of revelation by a grace-enlightened intellect working, in so far as possible, up to its full capacities. No superficial explanation can suffice, no premature cry of "mystery" can be allowed to stifle investigation. Obviously, then, the student's philosophical principles will guide his theological thinking, and diverse philosophies will produce theologies that differ according to divergencies.

Within the broad stream of scholasticism there run various currents of Catholic theology, all derived from the same source and all heading toward the same outlet, but each somewhat different from the other currents. In this book we shall oversimplify these currents by distinguishing them as Thomistic, Suarezian and Scotistic—the first-named dividing into two sub-currents when it comes upon a great rock in midstream, the explanation of the hypostatic union.

Common Data

Concerning the Christian faith, all Catholic theologians (and many who are not Catholics) are in agreement. Christ is both God and man, and he is completely each one. Only the Son became incarnate; the Trinity is the efficient cause of the union, just as it is the cause of creation. The union is 93 substantial (that is, not merely accidental, as between two friends who remain distinct substances) but personal; the two natures belong to the one person, God the Son. There is a distinction, then, between "person" and "nature"; they are not the same. Any explanation given of the manner of this mysterious union is bound to remain incomplete; the hypostatic union is a mystery. It will remain so until the end of this book and longer. Otherwise, you are either dead and in heaven or a heretic. So keep it a mystery!

Is it worth while to propose *any* explanation of it, then? Can any good come of spending time on something so exalted that we know beforehand we shall not understand it adequately until we reach the beatific vision? Surely yes, if by our study we come to know more about Christ, if we penetrate deeper into the reality of God's love which is personally manifested to us by the God-man in his person and in his life. Even though we cannot know all about this mystery, we do know much already. We can come to know much more by following the thoughts of the Church's theologians as well as we can.

The Problem

The problem is clear: How can it be that Christ is only one person, if he is truly human as well as divine? Why is he not a human person, too? Or, if he is omniscient, omnipotent, and ubiquitous, how can he also be nescient, weak, localized? Can such seemingly contradictory qualities really belong to the same one thing? Is it possible that both sets can be preserved and unity retained? To answer such questions, theological theories are proposed.

It is not as though the matter were completely mysterious. To serve as analogies we know various unities resulting from combinations of unlikely partners: soul and body to form one man, for instance. What a wondrous thing is man. A little less than the angels, yet at times little more than a beast. A spirited body, an enfleshed angel. Only God could think of such a thing. We know the truth of the reality from personal experience of ourselves. What, then, of a God-man? Is such a combination impossible to the wisdom and power of God? We know the answer to this question, too, but only by faith and because he has told us of it. We have no direct experience of such a combination except in the mirror of our faith. We hope to see him as he is, with the help of his glory's light, in heaven.

For now, we must use earthly comparisons: fire glowing in what had been dusty charcoal bricklets, last week's hamburgers now intussuscepted into our bodies, nectarines, tigrons, ligers and army "ducks" (trucks amphibious, not fowl). We know of such unities-from-diversity, and distinguish the two types: substantial unity that produces existing *things* and accidental unity that simply modifies already existing substances, for instance thoughts coming to our minds, even in class, or the present position of our bodies—prone, perhaps. We can deduce that the union of God and man in Christ is substantial in the sense of not accidental, permanent and not transient, in his very being and not merely external like clothing or locality. The Word did not merely wear his humanity like a scuba outfit, however form-fitting such may be. He was and is human; the union must be expressed in terms of his *being,* if it is to be a theological theory.

Toward an Answer

The general question, then, is: why is Jesus Christ only one person? The initial answer, which corresponds to the question of fact rather than to reason for the fact, is that through his Church he teaches that he is. All theologians begin their explanation by saying that the human nature of Christ lacks whatever constitutes human personality (in the philosophical sense). Only the second person, the Word, gives personality to Christ. Probably all would agree that this person-factor in Christ, as in any person, is "incommunicable"—a term that carries overtones of "independence, individuality, totality-in-itself, intellectual self-consciousness, responsibility, conscience." Human nature does not a person make, but only a human. Christ is human, but not a human person.

Nature versus Person

One more example is appropriate. If there are thirty students seated in a classroom before an instructor, there are thirty-one human natures, and thirty-one human persons present. If Christ came through that door, visible to the eye, there would be thirty-two human natures here and thirty-one human persons, and one divine person. If what we have said is true, human nature cannot automatically mean human person; there must be some difference between them. How do we know this? From revelation only, as we have seen at length in our chapters on the Bible. No wonder the apostles were so slow to understand what Jesus was telling them.

Still the question arises, "Was the Son of God human from all eternity?" If not, then he certainly was not a human person before the incarnation, whether he was after it or not. But he was a person, the second person of the Trinity, so he did not become a person in 6 B.C. or whenever he was conceived. He is still that same divine person, enjoying the infinite reality of God. He is not merely a human person, then. The Fathers made this a favored theme: "Without ceasing to be what he was (God), he became what he was not (man)."

He has a human nature, then. He has whatever it is that makes us human, men instead of monkeys or maple trees. "Human nature" may not be a completely clear philosophical concept, but is sufficiently distinct for us to use it as the Church uses it. Christ is man, totally and integrally; he did not become angel or animal-vegetable-mineral of the parlor game. He has a rational soul and human body, like us. He is human—but probably it is better   95 not to call him "a human being." The reason why it is preferable not to lies in a somewhat arbitrary choice of language, following out the theological opinion that seems best to the present writer.

CAPREOLUS

That opinion is usually attributed to a Dominican theologian named Capreolus, sometimes referred to as "Prince of Thomists." In this theory, any actually existing being is made up of two elements: the nature or essence, and its proper act of being. These two are really distinct; one is not the other. Together, they immediately constitute a real and actual thing, a being. You are a being, then, because your individual human nature is joined to its own proper and proportionate act of being; the result is *you*. Your act of being is commensurate with your nature; it is human being . . . John Dough's being. It makes you *a* human being, *this* human being. All right so far? If not, go back, friend, go back. Ask your instructor to go over it again. And think. Don't try now to imagine this theory, or to draw an outline of it. Theories are for thinking, as subways are for sleeping.

Now to apply this theory on being to Christ. From eternity he is the second divine person, utterly perfect and unchanging in his godhead. In time this Son of God takes to himself an individual human nature from Mary, not ceasing to be the second person or losing anything of his godhead thereby. Capreolus' theory would say: This human nature lacks its own proper act of merely human being, but enjoys a share in an infinitely superior act of being, the Being of the Son of God himself. This share in the eternal Being of the Son, then, does duty for what would be a merely human act of being of the human nature by giving actuality to that human nature. Far from being less human as a result, the body-soul combination of Christ is raised to absolute perfection precisely as human because of the surpassing grace given to his human nature. This is the grace of personal union with the Son of God. Christ's human mind is the keenest of minds for it is God's human mind; his human will is freest, for it is God's human will. His human "being" is really not merely human; it derives its ultimate reality from its sharing the filial Being of God's Son. For this reason, it seems better to say that Christ is human or a human (and some would even question this), but not a human being.

CAJETAN

Another Dominican Thomist, Cajetan, proposes a slightly different explanation, and is followed by many modern members of his religious order as well as by numerous other theologians. He holds for a real distinction between nature or essence and the act of being, of course, but demands one other thing for personality: a mode of subsistence added to the nature (essence) to dispose it for that proper act of being that gives it actuality. Human subsistence, then, is what Christ's human nature is missing, with the result that it is not a human person. Instead, his human nature by the marvel of hypostatic union is drawn into the subsistence of the divine Son. One difficulty with this theory, and the reason why Capreolus' theory seems preferable, is that if such a mode of subsistence is necessary for human nature before it can exist, then it is essential to human nature as such. Christ, in lacking such a human mode, is lacking something essential to human nature, and is not what we are. Obviously, those who prefer this theory of Cajetan would not admit this criticism. The matter is one of free opinion, remember.

SUAREZ

Still another theory is drawn from Francis Suarez, S.J., a commentator on St. Thomas as Cajetan and Capreolus were. Denying the real distinction between nature or essence and the act of being in creatures (thereby incurring the displeasure of those who consider this thesis "a fundamental principle of the science of God as well as of any true philosophy") ,* Suarez explained the mystery of Christ in much the same way as Cajetan had—through a mode of subsistence which must be added to the nature-being in order to constitute an actual person. Christ does not have this human mode of subsistence, so he is not a human person. He does, however, have a real human existing nature. The difficulty with this theory, of course, is in its philosophical presuppositions which must be accepted before the theory can be accepted. Not many are to be found who are convinced of the compelling force of his philosophical imperative.

SCOTUS

The final theory we shall consider is called Scotistic, after the Franciscan theologian Duns Scotus. The human nature of Christ is not a human person because God assumed that human nature. You and I are human persons because God has *not* assumed our human natures. It is as simple as that. This oversimplification, no doubt does not attain the subtleties of Scotus' complete theory, but it seems to express its central contention.

The difficulty found with it is that it tells us little more than we already knew. Nonassumption of the nature hardly seems an adequate explanation of so rich a reality as personality; the humanness would be exactly the same in the nonpersonal nature of Christ as in the personal humanness of you and me—just the same and just as actual, for according to Scotus, Christ's human nature would automatically become a human person (different from Christ, of course) if the Son of God ceased to assume it. Nothing would need to be added; the nature-being of Christ would immediately exist as a person, a new person. This seems to mean that in the God-man there would really be two

---

* T. Donlan and others, *Christ and His Sacraments* (Dubuque, Iowa: Priory Press, 1958).

complete beings, and in such case hardly united in one and the same Jesus Christ. For this reason, Scotism has been compared to the Antioch-approach of Chapter Eight, with its making sure of the real humanity of the God-man. Similarly, the Thomist solution has been compared with the Alexandrian approach, in that it emphasizes the divine unity of Christ.

THE MYSTERY OF THE HYPOSTATIC UNION

Whichever of these theories the student may elect to hold as more probable and hence preferable, he should know wherein he situates the mystery of the hypostatic union, and why. The grace of union communicates the eternal being of the Son to the created nature born of Mary. This communication is a grace of personal union given to the nature; it is the most marvelous of graces. Unlike sanctifying grace of adoptive sonship in us, it makes the human nature belong personally to the natural Son of God. St. Thomas says of it:

> The grace of union is the personal being that is given gratis from above to the human nature in the Person of the Word, and is the term of the assumption. . . . This man (as a result of the union) is the Only-begotten of the Father. . . . (S. Th. 3,6,6)

> Thus, since the human nature is united to the Son of God hypostatically or personally . . . and not accidentally, it follows that by the human nature there accrued to Him no new personal being, but only a new relation of the pre-existing personal being to the human nature, in such a way that the Person is said to subsist not merely in the Divine, but also in the human nature. (3,17,2)

> The eternal being of the Son of God, which is the Divine Nature, becomes the being of man, inasmuch as the human nature is assumed by the Son of God to unity of Person. (3,17,2, ad 2)

Go back now, and see which theory best fits the saint's ideas. Pick one, and hold fast the mystery!

Christ's Human Knowledge

Earlier in this chapter we said that Christ's human mind is keenest, for it is God's human mind. His neighbors caught some idea of this in their contacts with him which drew from them remarks like, "Never did man speak like this," or "Where did he learn, for he never went to school?" He called himself "truth"; his insights are still the common inheritance of all men. How could it be otherwise, if he is God incarnate? Would he not possess all types of human knowledge necessary for the accomplishment of his messianic mission?

The Fathers distinguished his knowledge only as divine or human, perfect or imperfect—and perhaps we would be better off if we did only as much as they. Be that as it may, we have come to distinguish three general types: knowledge drawn from ordinary human experience, called experiential knowledge; knowledge derived from Christ's personal intuition of his own being, called beatific because the blessed in heaven have it from their grace of beatific vision; knowledge given him directly by God but not through vision, called infused. All of us have experiential knowledge, and grow in it each moment. The saints in heaven have vision of the Word. The first man must have had infused knowledge of intellectual ideas at his creation, in order to know what to do as an adult. It is only fitting that the God-man during his mortal life should have all three types of knowledge (if they be three), for he is superior to and head of all men. Moreover, in a certain sense he needed all three types.

EXPERIENTIAL KNOWLEDGE   The first type of knowledge seems obvious enough. The day-to-day experience of being Mary's child, a growing boy and man, a Jew of Nazareth and then of Jerusalem—brought constant new knowledge to his mind and soul. He "learned obedience" as well as his Aleph-Beth-Ghimels, and how to work with a craftsman's hands in Joseph's shop. Strangely enough, St. Thomas for a long time thought Christ did not so learn. He changed his opinion by the end of his life, however, and admitted it, humble scholar that he was. (S.Th. 3,9,4; cf. 3 Sent., 14,3.) His chief reason for changing was the need he felt for the mind of Christ to be active, and not merely a passive tool in the clutch of the divine mind. The Child grew in wisdom, grew in the manifestation of the truth that was in him, grew in Israel's culture and Nazareth's way. He was a Jew of his time; God became *this* man, son of Mary, resident of Galilee.

BEATIFIC KNOWLEDGE   The second occasions some difficulties at first. Beatific vision is the goal of all human striving, not an aid to mortal living. To see all truth in the Word of God who is truth is the privilege of those who have fought the good fight and have attained heaven. They are no longer exposed to suffering and doubt; they have won through to the reward promised to those who are faithful to the end. Yet how fitting it is that Christ should possess this vision from his first moment on earth. He must have been conscious of who he was, in each intellectual act he performed. The person thinking, reaching up for Mary's finger from the crib, choosing death for our sakes rather than back down before the pharisees; this person is truth himself, through whom all things were made—as Paul says, all things visible and invisible. (Col 1,15f) How could he not know in himself all there was to know? If the saints know all things somehow, in beatific vision, then surely Christ in intuiting his own self must know the same.

But the difficulty! Could he have such vision before his death, above all at times when he felt sorrowful, disappointed, angry, or tearful? "My God, my God, why have you abandoned me?" This is not the cry of one enjoying the   *99* beatific vision.

Quite right. Not of one "enjoying" the vision, perhaps, but of one having it in a way different from the "beatific" way of the blessed. The gospels clearly show Christ as subject to many limitations of body, and we take them for granted: hunger, thirst, weariness. We also admit limitations in his soul: disappointment, sorrow, fear. To limit his full enjoyment of the vision of reality until after his mortal life is over seems consistent with his state of true mortal humanness and meriting. According to this theory, then, he had in his human faculties the knowledge of vision, but not the connatural, postjudgment effect(s) of that knowledge: perfect joy of body and soul. He knew past-present-future, everything and everyone connected with his messianic mission; he knew it in his vision of himself, the Word of God. But in God's providence this knowledge during his earthly life ordinarily served only to inform him, not to give him the actual perfect "joy" of heaven.

Did he really know "the day and the hour," then? (Mk 13,32) It would seem that he would have to. Heretics called Agnoetae claimed that he did not. St. Gregory the Great remarked that they were themselves completely ignorant about Christ's ignorance, for only a Nestorian could believe that the God-man was truly ignorant of such an important matter. His mission simply did not include revelation of that interesting item, that is all, possibly because such confusion attended the notion in his own day.

Such a vision of all human reality assured the truth of Christ's judgments and words. We need not make our Lord the greatest nuclear physicist that ever lived, or the most learned mathematician, any more than we must make him the best athlete or the handsomest man. Such idealizing runs the risk of dehumanizing him and losing him in the vagueness of Monophysitism. The so-called principle of perfection does apply to him in many ways, and we ought to find in him all that goes to make up perfect manhood and the perfect man, redeemer and head of the human race. But surely a principle of imperfection also has place, and acts as a healthy counterbalance to unauthorized imaginings about a divinized man. In this matter of the human knowledges of Christ, both principles must be adequately influential.

INFUSED KNOWLEDGE   The third human type of knowledge is the infused or instinctive—the result of neither experience nor the vision common to the blessed. It results from light given to Christ's mind directly by God, so that he could express in human terms the divine mysteries revealed to him in that inexpressible vision. With this knowledge he could reflect on his vision and say, "Before Abraham was, I am." With this knowledge, he could foreknow the physical pains of his passion and break into a bloody sweat in Gethsemani on the evening before his death. With this knowledge, he could foreknow and feel abandonment by his beloved disciples, betrayal by Judas, rejection by his own Israel and by each sin of each man. It is the basis for the theological explanation of personal reparation to the Sacred Heart, for he also foreknew each man's repentant efforts to make up for past sins.

Pope Pius XI seems to have had such infused knowledge in mind when he wrote:

> And if, in view of our own future sins, foreseen by Him, the soul of Jesus became sad even unto death, there can be no doubt that by His prevision at the same time of our act of reparation He was in some way comforted when "there appeared an angel from heaven" [Lk 22,43] to console that heart of his bowed down with sorrow and anguish. (*Miserentissimus Redemptor,* No. 15)

This infused knowledge, then, was not by nature beatific, and could easily be combined with the experience of sorrow, pain, almost despair. But its main function was to enable the human mind of our Lord to put into human terms the marvels of God's mysteries revealed to him in vision. "No one knows the Father but the Son, and he to whom the Son reveals him." (Mt 11,27) Without this infused knowledge, the newness that marked Christ's teachings would have been seriously curtailed, at the outset of his career, until his experiential knowledge grew greater through his gradual study of the Scriptures and Israel's expectations. With it, he astonished the doctors in the Temple as well as his mother, and earned the title that men naturally accorded him from the beginning of his ministry—"the Teacher."

Christ's Human Freedom

So much for his human mind, then; his human will is the other faculty marking him out as truly man. Existentialist philosophers have renewed the centrality of the freedom of man in any analysis of an individual's or a nation's history. Freedom is the rallying cry around our world. In a real sense, Christ died for freedom—freedom from the tyranny of sin, death, and the devil. Freely he chose the passion, for thus he merited the graces of redemption for us all as the Council of Trent has taught. (D799) Freedom he had himself, sovereign freedom as became the Lord of heaven and earth, to whom all power was given. "He chose whom he would himself." (Mk 3,13) The Fathers loved to dwell on the theme that his mission on earth was to heal and guide man's sick, distorted free will; for this, he had to be free himself. "What he did not assume, he did not heal" applied above all to freedom.

But how was he free? You know that human freedom is explained in various ways by various philosophers. Whatever theory of ultimate human freedom you find sensible and consistent you should apply to the free will of Christ. Any theory will ensure his ability to control his choices, for in such dominion over our actions truly human freedom consists. Neither external force nor internal determination may be allowed to cancel out the individual's power to choose between alternatives, whether those alternatives be good-or-bad, or good-or-better. No communist type "freedom" is in question here, the "collective freedom" of individuals to conform their wills to the party line. All theories consistent with Catholic faith will preserve a man's responsibility for his own decisions, for good or ill. You need to follow one, and be consistent about it.

A sense of freedom is the most Godlike of man's gifts, for it enables him to be like God in acting independently of and in his environment. The price everyone pays, however, is proportionate to the gift. We may freely reject both God and godliness through sin, and some may, like Satan, have paid the ultimate penalty by choosing the hell of self-love for eternity. Christ's freedom is different from ours in this, for not only did he not sin but he *could* not sin. Sin, moral evil, hatred of God—this simply had no place in the life of the God-man; he who was God could not hate himself, nor could a human will hypostatically united to the godhead choose against the perfect God. "He was like to us in all things, sin alone excepted." (Heb 4,15) The message to Mary announced him as the Holy One of Israel (Lk 1,35) whose mission it was to destroy sin. Sinfulness, therefore, had no place in him, although temptation from without did. In the desert and in the garden he endured the assaults of his enemy, teaching us that such external trials need by no means be sinful and can be the means of meriting. The holiness of his moral life was perfect, for he had not the least inclination to sin; no uncontrolled emotion even momentarily threw him off balance. The holiness of Jesus has been a constant wonder to readers of the New Testament; many have found in his sinlessness the best proof of his godhead, for no mere man could be so good, so self-sacrificing, so uniquely intent on doing God's will. To err is human; to forgive, divine. Jesus needed no forgiveness, for no moral error crept into his life. "Father, forgive *them* . . ." is the measure of his holiness and love.

And yet his very sinlessness occasions a problem for us in assessing his freedom. In St. John's gospel we read:

> For this reason the Father loves me, because I lay down my life that I may take it up again. No one takes it from me, but I lay it down of myself. I have the power to lay it down, and I have the power to take it up again. Such is the command I have received from my Father. (Jn 10,17f)

The passion-resurrection, then, seems to be commanded by the Father, and we have the problem: if Christ was unable to sin, and was commanded to die, was he still free to die? Even worse, was he free *not* to die? If he was not free, then his death was not meritorious—an impossibility. *Voilà* and *eccolo!* This has been called the "Thermopylae of theology." It leaves precious little room through which to squeeze a sufficient explanation.

Christ seems to have had a true command from his Father, although some have avoided the worst of the difficulty by interpreting the Greek word as meaning only a sign of God's preference, not a strict precept binding morally. Some say that even with a strict command, the sinless Christ could obey it freely because it concerned a less-than-total good, his passion with its sufferings; therefore it left room for freedom in the human will choosing this limited good according to the created nature of human freedom. Many say that he was not free in regard to the object of the command, but was free concerning the means of fulfilling it or the circumstances surrounding it.

AN ANSWER   Taking the latter position, we have only to decide on the object of the Father's command. If it was Christ's death, then his freedom did not concern this, but operated primarily in choosing the details of the passion. Since the biblical revelation seems to make the whole paschal event (suffering-death-resurrection-ascension) the meritorious cause and exemplar of our redemption, however, it seems better to consider this as freely chosen by Christ, and to make the Father's command concern some more general precept. This thinking underlies the explanation suggested below.

The Father's command was a general one such as: "Save the world," or "Manifest our love for men," or "Restore eternal life to men." (Cf. Jn 12,49f.) For this he is sent, and he is not free to say no. (His divine will, of course, is supremely free in decreeing this command to be fulfilled by Christ on earth, but this is not the point; we are concerned here with his human freedom only.) His human freedom, then, comes to bear upon the paschal event as the best means of implementing this command. For love of us, and out of his all-consuming love for his Father, he chooses to obey "even until death, even to the death of the cross." (Phil 2,8f) *Therefore* God exalted him, rewarding his obedient love with honors due to God alone. From the first moment of his conscious life he made this choice, and carried it out steadfastly in Nazareth, Capharnaum, Galilee, and Judea until the day he finally set his face for the last time toward Jerusalem, to meet the disgrace and glory of his passion.

What are we to make of the inner struggle in the garden, then? Only this: that he was completely human, and that the anticipation of awful agonies of body and soul affected his human emotions just as similar things do ours. Anticipated pain is ordinarily worse than the reality. Imminent danger is quite different from remote danger.

In Gethsemani our Lord's feelings were outraged by the prevision in detail of all his imminent sufferings—physical and mental—and caused that amazing cry, "Father, if it be possible, let this cup pass away from me." (Mt 26,39) His will, however, remained completely set on that of his Father. "Yet not as I will, but as you will." (*Ibid.*) He freely chose not only to suffer in so many ways and to die, but also to suffer from this outrage of his feelings; the harmony of his human free will with his Father's will was perfect. He was the Second Adam, restoring by his obedience the possibility of holiness for all mankind.

MODERN THEOLOGIZING

Present-day theologians are reflecting on these aspects of Christology, bringing to the usual interpretations the new insights continually being gained from biblical, historical, and liturgical studies. The Church's task in our day is, as always, to proclaim the central mystery of Christ within the context of the present. She may not be content with mere rote memory of words from the past. In making the proclamation, however, she keeps clearly to the biblical message and the faith committed once for all to Christ's mystical body on earth. This faith does not change, although the manner of presenting it may, and does vary in the formulas used to express it as well as the languages. Some formulas have been rejected, as false to the revelation of the Word. "Christ as man is the adopted son of God" is a good instance of this. "Christ is one person with two natures" is the Chalcedonic definition of faith, crystallizing the data of revelation concerning who and what the God-man is.

Modern theologians try to make this formula more and more meaningful in terms of modern thought. The danger is that it may become merely a formula, whereas it ought to be the expression of the reality by which we live and hope to die. The particular danger felt today is the extreme emphasis on the divinity of Jesus so that a real humanity is either lost or ignored. As person, he is God the Son. Yet the persons we know are human beings, human persons. If Christ is not a human person, is he truly real for us? When we say, "In Christ, God walked the earth," do we have the same understanding of the phrase that we have when we read in Genesis that God was walking in the garden in the cool of the day? If so, then the incarnation is quite unreal to us, and Chalcedon's defense of the human *phýsis* of Christ as itself operative has not taken hold of our minds.

Yet the revelation seems clearer than clear. The manhood of Christ is real, and it determined his human life just as his godhead determined his divine activities. His prayer, submissive to the Father's will, is empty posturing unless the creatureliness of Christ is allowed its full meaning. That he *became* Lord . . . that he was *raised* by God . . . that he *emptied* himself . . . that the *man* Christ Jesus is the one mediator—such aspects of the revelation must be seen as equally valuable for our understanding and faith as "I and the Father are one" and "He is the image of the invisible God." His earthly, human life must be for us the mediatorial activity that historically saves us. St. Thomas and Suarez included the mysteries of the life of Christ in their Christologies; moderns seldom do so, perhaps because the biblical scholars have not yet clarified these mysteries sufficiently to permit a dependable theological treatment of them.

Work is being done on this, of course, as a glance at the journals listed in the bibliography for this chapter amply demonstrates. But we still need to know much more about what happened at the transfiguration, for instance, and how the hidden life causes the graces of our daily lives. Christ's historical life must be the permanent law of man's life, the life of individuals, of the Church, and of the entire world; it cannot be the object merely of Christian piety or defensive apologetics. Odo Casel's theory of the presence of Calvary in each Mass offers interesting possibilities for the other events of Christ's life. We need repeated epiphanies of Christ in our own days; as members of his body, we need to find the meaning of our own daily lives in the salvific exemplar of completely human life: the historic life of Jesus, sign of how near man can come to God in daily human life, because it *is* God's human life.

The technical word for this latter reality is "theandric" (*theós,* God, and the Greek word for man). Jesus is the unique God-man whose every act expressed the complete and personal penetration of human life by God the Son. Jesus *is* the God-man; what he does, God the Son does. The moral value of these "theandric" acts is therefore unlimited, for they belong to the beloved Son in whom the Father was well-pleased. For this we his members are grateful, as well as proud.

Questions

Some questions that are being asked include the following. How does the absolute changelessness of God affect our belief in the incarnation? If the Word *became* man, was he not somehow different after it happened? Is Christ truly the apex of creation, the goal of all human history, if he lived so long ago? And of course if human life continues for some thousands of millennia the problem will be set in higher relief. Why must there be only one incarnation of God—could there not be another or others in the future— possibly of the Holy Spirit or of the Father? Can we understand what man is without including Christ? Is anthropology in a sense a "deficient Christology," and Christology a "transcendent anthropology"? How may one explain the unity of consciousness of the one Christ with his three types of knowledge? Above all, how explain his human consciousness of his own godhead— of the infinite person that he was? Some theologians say this came through his beatific vision, whereas others hold it came through some other divine-human means as yet unclear to us.

These are some of the theological questions being asked and some of the problems being investigated. Tentative answers are being formulated, tentative solutions suggested. Meanwhile, God's Spirit commits the Church to full faith in Christ, the fullness of God's revelation to men; she continues to give that faith to her children, secure in the belief that it is permanent and unchanging, glad that her theologians are constantly seeking new and better ways for her to proclaim that saving message to men.

CHAPTER TEN

MY LORD
AND MY GOD

"Thomas answered and said to him, 'My Lord and my God.' Jesus said to him, 'Because you have seen me, Thomas, you have believed. Blessed are they who have not seen, and yet have believed.'" (Jn 20,29) This is Christ's final beatitude on us all, for John's gospel originally ended at Chapter 20. Surely we all qualify for this last benediction, for we have not seen him in the days of his flesh, nor heard his voice speaking to calm our fears. Yet we join Thomas in confessing his Lordship and Godhead, in believing that he is in truth the Savior sent into the world. Do we now believe more firmly and with greater awareness?

You might well reread Chapter One now to see what you were promised in this book. What do you think of Christ now that you have finished it? Do you think any more, or perhaps more clearly, about him? Do you understand yourself and your own human life any better for having spent this time studying the God-man? You should revere and respect your human nature more now, if you have really understood the meaning of his incarnation. Your body has been sanctified by his body; Christmas will remind you of this—and so will your communions with Christ now living in a glorious body.

Why will you go to church now—and how? Is it still only routine and rote, or do you now see that you are answering a call and a challenge? *God* awaits you in church. God *incarnate* awaits you. The glorified Victim of Calvary and heaven awaits you. In the television play of Graham Greene's *The Power and the Glory,* the whiskey-priest murmurs wonderingly but certainly, "I can put God in a man's mouth," and goes back to face death for the sake of God's people. Do we yet understand?

Does Christ have the answers for our nuclear world? Surely he does. He came, "that they may have life, and have it more abundantly." (Jn 10,10) He came to show his infinite love for man, for men, for us, for you. He came to give of himself, to show supreme self-giving of the Word in uniting a human nature to himself personally . . . to show infinite self-giving in first loving us when we were yet sinners. He is the goal of all our striving for union with God, the example of what grace can do to and for our humanness.

The film *La Dolce Vita* has been called a searing condemnation of a reversed incarnation: the flesh made word. The surrender of divinized flesh to the devil and the world is the perversion of all that God's incarnation means, and ends in emptiness. True incarnation leads to the exaltation of that very flesh, and its joyful perfection. Mary's "fiat" brought God's love enfleshed in Jesus, her son and God's son; a man's fiat to self-love brings only the misery of isolated hatefulness.

Our fiat must be like Mary's, to bring Christ into the world of our day. He must be incarnate in every generation of Christians, for the salvation of the world. We are members of his body, his mystical body now, and cannot be indifferent to the rest of the world. Our life must be a specifically Christian life, filled with Christian faith and hope and charity, urging us on to Christian works of love and mercy. These works are possible for all of us to some extent, as we come aware of the social problems of our world. Can we be self-centered and claim to be like Christ? careless of others, and say we follow him? aimless in life, and call ourselves Christians? Hardly.

For youth so many vistas of Christian life are open. The Peace Corps, the Papal Volunteers for Latin America, marriage and family life, the various social services, religious and priestly life, the teacher's vocation, work with the

Confraternity of Christian Doctrine, secular institutes, medical missions, parish societies that work for the poor and the afflicted—these are some of the opportunities offered in our times. The life of Christ's grace within a man must conform him to the Son of God, as an image and in imitation of him who gave himself for the life of the world.

"He who would save his life, will lose it; but he who loses his life for my sake and for the gospel's sake will save it." (Mk 8,35) In Christ we see the heights to which our human nature can be raised. He can raise us even higher than we are now. He is God's word, spoken to us once and for all time, yet speaking to us still; in prayer, public and private, we listen to his word.

Do all men hear his word? Many do. Poets praise Jesus Christ; artists strive to portray him as well as they can. Philosophers meditate on him; theologians kneel in thoughtful adoration of him. Scientists like Teilhard de Chardin construct cosmic syntheses around him as their center and solution. Meanwhile in the quiet of our rooms or in a sacred place, we gaze upon his symbol: the Crucified with the pierced heart. "Have confidence; I have overcome the world." (Jn 16,33)

In our personal lives, known to him alone, we must be different now—at least in our habitual thinking about this world that is his and ours. "My Lord and my God" must have some effect on us; otherwise it is meaningless sound and senseless symbol.

Perhaps we shall manifest this new attitude above all at Mass, in the communion especially, when we acknowledge his Lordship so often in the words of Mother Church. *Kyrie, eleison . . . Christe, eleison . . . Gloria in excelsis Deo . . . Domine, Fili unigenite, Jesu Christe . . . Tu solus sanctus . . . Gloria tibi, Domine . . . Credo in unum Deum . . . et in Jesum Christum filium Dei unigenitum . . . consubstantialem Patri . . . et homo factus est . . . cujus regni non erit finis . . . mirabilius reformasti . . . per Christum Dominum nostrum . . . Sanctus, Sanctus, Sanctus . . . hoc est enim corpus meum . . . calix sanguinis mei . . . per ipsum et cum ipso et in ipso est tibi, Pater, in unitate Spiritus Sancti, omnis honor et gloria . . . Agnus Dei, miserere nobis . . . dona nobis pacem . . . corpus Domini nostri Jesu Christi custodiat animam tuam in vitam aeternam . . . Ecce agnus Dei . . . in principio erat Verbum . . . et Deus erat Verbum . . . in propria venit et Sui eum non receperunt . . . et Verbum caro factum est, et habitavit in nobis . . . plenum gratiae et veritatis . . .* Sacred Heart of Jesus, have mercy on us.

What am I to say and think? One answer might be a prayer like that of St. Ignatius Loyola:

Dearest Lord, teach me to be generous. . . .
To give and not to count the cost,
To fight and not to mind the wounds,
To toil and not to seek for rest,
To labor and not to ask for reward
Save that of knowing that I am doing thy will.

May my greatest victories for you be achieved
In the cheerful, perfect performance of my daily duties.

The first ending of St. John's gospel goes like this:

Many other signs also Jesus worked in the sight of his disciples,
which are not written in this book. But these are written that you may
believe that Jesus is the Christ, the Son of God, and that believing,
you may have life in his name. (Jn 20,30f)

Selected Readings

CHAPTER TWO

Encyclicals mentioned in the text.

Any good missal, that, is one containing the restored order of Holy
Week in its entirety.

Adam, K., *The Christ of Faith* (New York: Pantheon, 1957), Ch. 1.

Chesterton, G. K., *The Everlasting Man* (New York: Doubleday
Image Books, 1960).

Fremantle, A., *The Papal Encyclicals* (New York: Mentor Books,
1956). Foreword by G. Weigel, on "The Significance of Papal
Pronouncements," pp. 9-20.

O'Shea, W., *The Worship of the Church* (Westminster, Md.: Newman, 1957).

Suhard, E., *The Church Today* (Chicago: Fides, 1953).

CHAPTER THREE

Carol, J., *Mariology* (Milwaukee: Bruce), 1954, Vol. I, pp. 1-50,
80-107, 328-394; 1957, Vol. II, pp. 177-312; 1961, Vol. III, pp.
1-21, 422-439.

DeVaux, R., *Ancient Israel* (New York: McGraw-Hill, 1962), pp.
100-114, 312-357, 484-517.

Gelin, A., and others, *Son and Saviour* (Baltimore: Helicon, 1960),
Ch. I.

Houselander, C., *The Reed of God* (New York: Sheed and Ward,
1944).

McKenzie, J. L., *The Two-Edged Sword* (Milwaukee: Bruce, 1956).

Pius IX, *Ineffabilis Deus* ("The Immaculate Conception").

Robert, A., and A. Tricot, *Guide to the Bible* (New York: Desclee),
Vol. I (rev.) 1960; Vol. II, 1955.

CHAPTER FOUR

Cullmann, O., *The Christology of the New Testament* (Philadelphia: Westminster, 1959).

Gelin, A., and others, *Son and Saviour* (Baltimore: Helicon, 1960), Ch. 3.

Kleist, J., and J. Lilly, *The New Testament* (Milwaukee: Bruce, 1956).

Lagrange, M. J., *The Gospel of Jesus Christ*, Vols. I-II (New York: Benziger, 1952).

New Testament Reading Guide (Collegeville, Minn.: Liturgical Press, 1960), No. 1: *Introduction to the New Testament* (R. A. F. McKenzie); No. 2: *The Gospel of St. Mark* (G. Sloyan).

Taylor, V., *The Gospel According to St. Mark* (London: Macmillan, 1959).

CHAPTER FIVE

Gelin, A., and others, *Son and Saviour* (Baltimore: Helicon, 1960), Chs. 2 and 3.

New Testament Reading Guide (Collegeville, Minn.: Liturgical Press, 1960), No. 3: The Gospel According to St. Luke (C. Stuhlmueller); No. 4: The Gospel According to St. Matthew (D. Stanley); No. 5: The Acts of the Apostles (N. Flanagan).

Taylor, V., *The Person of Christ in New Testament Teaching* (London: Macmillan, 1958).

CHAPTER SIX

Gelin, A., *Son and Saviour* (Baltimore; Helicon, 1960), Chs. 4, 5.

New Testament Reading Guide (Collegeville, Minn.: The Liturgical Press, 1960), No. 7: Paul to the Romans and Galatians (B. Ahern); No. 8: Paul to the Corinthians, I,II (C. Peifer); No. 9: Paul to the Philippians, Colossians, Ephesians (K. Sullivan); No. 13: The Gospel According to St. John, and His Epistles (R. Brown).

CHAPTER SEVEN

Bettenson, H., *The Early Christian Fathers* (New York: Oxford University Press, 1956).

Daniélou, J., *Christ and Us* (New York: Sheed and Ward, 1961), Ch. 3.

Kelly, J. N. D., *Early Christian Doctrines* (New York: Harper, 1958).

Luke [Salm], Celestine, *Historical Christology* (New York: Manhattan College, 1959).

Quasten, J., *Patrology* (Westminster, Md.: Newman, 1949-1960), Vols. 1-3.

CHAPTER EIGHT

Clarkson, J., and others, *The Church Teaches: Documents of the Church in Translation* (St. Louis: B. Herder, 1955).

Hughes, Philip, *The Church in Crisis: A History of the General Councils,* 325-1870 (New York: Hanover House, 1961), pp. 1-144.

Pius XI, *Lux Veritatis* ("The Light of Truth") (Fifteenth Centenary of Ephesus) (Washington, D.C. NCWC, 1931).

Pius XII, *Orientalis Ecclesiae Decus* ("On Cyril of Alexandria") (Washington, D.C.: NCWC, 1944).

  , *Sempiternus Rex* ("Fifteenth Centenary of Chalcedon") (Washington, D.C.: NCWC, 1951).

CHAPTER NINE

Adam, K., *The Christ of Faith* (New York: Pantheon, 1957; Mentor Books, New American Library, 1962).

Aquinas, St. Thomas, *Summa Theologica,* translated by English Dominican Fathers (New York: Benziger, 1947), Vol. II, Third Part.

Clarke, T., "Current Christology," in *Thought* (Autumn, 1961), 325-43.

Daniélou, J., *Christ and Us* (New York: Sheed and Ward, 1961).

Donlan, T., and others, *Christ and His Sacraments* (Dubuque: Priory, 1958).

Henry, A., and others, *The Historical and Mystical Christ* (Chicago: Fides, 1958).

Héris, C., *The Mystery of Christ* (Westminster, Md.: Newman, 1950).

Mersch, E., *The Theology of the Mystical Body* (St. Louis, Herder, 1952).

Rahner, K., *Theological Investigations* (Baltimore: Helicon, 1961), Vol. I.

Scheeben, M., *The Mysteries of Christianity* (St. Louis: B. Herder, 1946).

Schlitzer, A., *Redemptive Incarnation,* 2nd rev. ed. (Notre Dame: University of Notre Dame Press, 1962).

Vonier, A., *Incarnation and Redemption* (London: Burns, Oates, Washburne, 1952).

Periodicals such as *Theology Digest, Theological Studies, Catholic Biblical Quarterly, Worship, Cross Currents, The Thomist, New Testament Abstracts, The Bible Today.*

ABBREVIATIONS

The Books of the Old and New Testaments

Genesis	Gn	Canticle of Canticles	Ct
Exodus	Ex	Wisdom	Wis
Leviticus	Lv	Sirach (Ecclesiasticus)	Sir
Numbers	Nm	Isaia	Is
Deuteronomy	Dt	Jeremia	Jer
Joshua	Jos	Lamentations	Lam
Judges	Jgs	Baruch	Bar
Ruth	Ru	Ezechiel	Ez
1 Samuel (1 Kings)	1 Sm	Daniel	Dn
2 Samuel (2 Kings)	2 Sm	Osea	Os
1 Kings (3 Kings)	1 Kgs	Joel	Jl
2 Kings (4 Kings)	2 Kgs	Amos	Am
1 Chronicles (Paralipomenon)	1 Chr	Abdia	Abd
2 Chronicles (Paralipomenon)	2 Chr	Jona	Jon
Ezra	Ez	Michea	Mi
Nehemia (2 Ezra)	Neh	Nahum	Na
Tobia	Tb	Habacuc	Hb
Judith	Jdt	Sophonia	So
Esther	Est	Aggai	Ag
Job	Jb	Zacharia	Za
Psalms	Ps(s)	Malachia	Mal
Proverbs	Prv	1 Machabees	1 Mc
Coheleth (Ecclesiastes)	Coh	2 Machabees	2 Mc

In the enumeration of the Psalms, the first number follows the Vulgate, the number within brackets, the Hebrew text.

St. Matthew	Mt	1 Timothy	1 Tim
St. Mark	Mk	2 Timothy	2 Tim
St. Luke	Lk	Titus	Ti
St. John	Jn	Philemon	Phlm
Acts of the Apostles	Ac	Hebrews	Heb
Romans	Rom	St. James	Jas
1 Corinthians	1 Cor	1 St. Peter	1 Pt
2 Corinthians	2 Cor	2 St. Peter	2 Pt
Galatians	Gal	1 St. John	1 Jn
Ephesians	Eph	2 St. John	2 Jn
Philippians	Phil	3 St. John	3 Jn
Colossians	Col	St. Jude	Jude
1 Thessalonians	1 Thes	Apocalypse	Ap
2 Thessalonians	2 Thes		

Apocrypha and Qumrân Material

Henoch	Hen	Testament of the	
Jubilees	Jub	Twelve Patriarchs	Test
Psalms of Solomon	Ps Sol	Manual of Discipline	MD

Other Source Material

Acta Apostolicae Sedis
 [Acts of the Apostolic See]   AAS
Ancient Christian Writers,
 ed. J. Quasten and others   ACW
Acta Sanctae Sedis
 [Acts of the Holy See]   ASS
Codex Iuris Canonici
 [Code of Canon Law]   CIC
Denzinger-Bannwart, Enchiridion
 Symbolorum, 30th ed. [Handbook
 of the Creeds]   D
Patrologia, series graeca,
 ed. J. P. Migne   PG

Sacrorum Conciliorum nova
 . . . Collectio   Mansi
Patrologia, series latina,
 ed. J. P. Migne   PL
Summa contra Gentes
 S. Thomae Aquinatis   S.C.G.
Quatuor Libri Sententiarum,
 Petri Lombardi [Four Books
 of Opinions]   Sent.
Summa Theologiae
 S. Thomae Aquinatis   S.Th.
The Church Teaches,
 ed. J. Clarkson and others   TCT

INDEX